DOOR TO THE RIVER

BY ARAM SAROYAN

POETRY

Poems (1972)
Day and Night: Bolinas Poems (1998)
Complete Minimal Poems (2007)

NOVELS AND STORIES

The Street: An Autobiographical Novel (1974)
The Romantic (1988)
Artists in Trouble: New Stories (2001)

NONFICTION

Genesis Angels: The Saga of Lew Welch and the Beat Generation
    (1979)
William Saroyan (1983)
Trio: Portrait of an Intimate Friendship (1985)
Rancho Mirage: An American Tragedy of Manners, Madness
    and Murder (1993)

MEMOIRS

Last Rites: The Death of William Saroyan (1982)
Friends in the World: The Education of a Writer (1992)

ESSAYS

Starting Out in the Sixties: Selected Essays (2001)

DOOR TO THE RIVER

Essays and Reviews from the 1960s into the Digital Age by ARAM SAROYAN

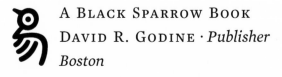

A BLACK SPARROW BOOK
DAVID R. GODINE · *Publisher*
Boston

This is
a Black Sparrow Book
first published in 2010 by
DAVID R. GODINE · *Publisher*
Post Office Box 450
Jaffrey, New Hampshire 03452
www.godine.com

LIBRARY OF CONGRESS
CATALOGING-IN-PUBLICATION DATA

Saroyan, Aram.
Door to the river : essays & reviews from the 1960s into the digital age /
by Aram Saroyan. — 1st ed.
p.   cm.
Includes bibliographical references.
ISBN 978-1-56792-396-4
I. Title.
PS3569.A72D66 2010
814'.54—dc22
2009022389

First Edition
PRINTED IN THE UNITED STATES OF AMERICA

CONTENTS

I knew that I, as an American, willy-nilly looked upon the president as one of the centers of my dream life. And it seemed to me that a lot of history is made in this country by the way that people react to their dream life. In other words, the shifts in public opinion come out of many elements that are not available to the historians. One of them is whether the president of the United States gives people energy in their inner lives, their dream lives, their unspoken lives. Or whether he takes it from them.

NORMAN MAILER
in a 1981 interview with
Barbara Probst Solomon

INTRODUCTION

THE EARLIEST PIECES in this book, in the final section, "Appendix: Beginnings," are among my first published writing, going back forty years to the mid-sixties, a lovely time in which to begin as a writer. I had dropped out of three colleges in two years and was on my literary way. The colleges, incidentally, had been in their various ways salutary experiences, but I was too restless for four years *anywhere*, let alone school. Nervous as I was, though, I was also paying attention as closely as I could manage, which the reader can take the measure of in "Beginnings." From the start, too, I was fairly eclectic – Creeley and Cheever, the *New York Review of Books* and Donovan, Giacometti and Ian Hamilton Finlay.

In the mid-seventies, I combined two primary affinities, poetry and a newly acquired competence in prose, having fortuitously discovered the book review devoted to the work of a familiar poet. For a year or so, I became a peripatetic voice in the field for the *New York Times Book Review*, the *Nation*, and the *Village Voice*. These days I tell my students not to be disdainful of the form, since, as I discovered, it's not a bad way to get a thought or two out into the daily discourse. Harvey Shapiro and Nona Balakian at the *Times*, Eliot Fremont-Smith at the *Village Voice*, and Emile Capouya at the *Nation* were all gracious to me, and I remain in their debt.

I stayed close to home in those seventies reviews – there's scarcely a poet I reviewed whom I hadn't met. Then I went through a decade of writing and publishing books – *Genesis Angels, Last Rites, William Saroyan, Trio, The Romantic* – during which my abilities were stretched and tested, and I acquired a practitioner's sense of what writing was actually about, though I might have been hard put to articulate it had anyone cared to ask.

In the essays that lead off here I reflect and elaborate on what the intervening years eventually brought me in the way of practical knowledge of the field and practice of creative prose, and they comprise a kind of bully pulpit, which by now had extended to the classroom. In these pieces I contend for what in my view comprises the good companionship that Jack Kerouac decreed was the true test of a book.

As a young writer I was lucky enough to find many lively peers at large in Manhattan and became a regular at the Wednesday night poetry readings at Café Le Metro off of St. Mark's Place. Ed Sanders, Ted Berrigan, Diane Wakoski, Jackson MacLow, Taylor Mead, Kathleen Fraser, Paul Blackburn, David Henderson, Ron Padgett, Gerard Malanga – the scene was a grab bag of styles and social strategies that was also generously welcoming. A poet named Dan Saxon passed around mimeo stencils and invited each poet to fill one up for his monthly magazine, *Poets at Le Metro*. Then too, more than a few of us started our own little magazines. It was a de facto poetry community – and an inspiring, no-holds-barred proving ground.

After all, a certain degree of arrogance may attend the normal birth rites of the aspiring writer – at least one not affiliated with either academia or the media. These days I'm surprised how many young writers are more or less professionally docile, dedicated worker bees, happy to find a place in the hive, and obligingly respectful and politic. The distance here from my own literary rites of passage may have to do with the received notion that the 1960s were a national, indeed an international aberration, for which all of us who took part in it paid a heavy price. This is mostly nonsense but it's the prevailing lore of our time and so one is obliged to acknowledge it. Crucially, the succeeding generation was thereby deprived of the lively gymnopedia that set me on my course as a writer.

The review of *The Collected Poems of Ted Berrigan* (2005) included here was turned down by the *London Review of Books* (for which I wrote it on spec), the *New York Times Book Review*, the *New York Review of Books*, and the *Los Angeles Times Book Review*, before being printed in 2008 by the *American Poetry Review*. So far as I know, it remains the only reasonably detailed consideration of the book to appear. Since Berrigan is one of a mere handful of recent American poets to whom I return with reliable pleasure, this tells me something isn't firing properly in our print media.

On the other hand, the blogs have done a lot to right the situation. In the interests of full disclosure, I should say that they played a decisive role in reviving my early minimal poetry. Then too I was surprised and touched when Ron Silliman, whose own blog is a leading purveyor of the literary business of the day, chose my *Complete Minimal Poems* (2007) for the Poetry Society of America's William Carlos Williams Award. When this was followed by a rave review by Richard Hell in the *New York Times Book Review*, it occurred to me that what I thought of as a paradigm shift from print to the web, which had made the book a poetry bestseller, had now reversed circuitry to show up in the hallowed pages of our newspaper of record. A nice synergy seemed to be in play.

Given my cordial relationship with a number of editors at the *Los Angeles Times*, I was disheartened after 9/11, when several pieces included here were summarily rejected for the op-ed page. The appalling eight years of the Bush administration were rarely relieved by a sense that our mainstream media was in working order, and, to press the point, one wonders if the quiescent character of so much political commentary didn't also date to the long-standing dismissal of the openness and candor of the 1960s. Which is to say that the forty-somethings running our magazines and newspapers seemed to be impersonating well-behaved children at a dinner party of power-crazed, drunken adults. It was as if there was an unspoken rule that no matter how outrageous things got, rigorous standards of collegial discourse needed to be maintained on the opinion pages. It fell to Senator Robert Byrd, in his eighties, to point out that the emperor had no clothes – or rather that he seemed not to have understood fundamental principles of decency.

It's clear that the new administration of President Barack Obama represents a passing of the torch, my own baby boom generation acceding to a cadre of public servants in marked contrast to any previous administration. Scarcely two years after assuming office as the

junior senator from Illinois, Mr. Obama declared his candidacy for
his party's nomination for president, though many of us barely
noticed it at the time. After all, Hillary Clinton, an extraordinary
politician by any measure, was the odds-on favorite for the Democratic Party's nomination. How did the fledgling candidate defeat so
strong and savvy a politician, and one with whom he shared many
common goals?

We can see now that the Obama team had a prescient understanding of the sea change introduced by the Internet, an understanding
that extended beyond the convenience of high-speed communication
to embrace a new sensibility. "The medium is the message," Marshall McLuhan famously advised; and more recently Lech Walesa
said that you could recognize the politics of the new generation in
its technology. Tellingly, our new president often refers to the
"information superhighway" and has made "unprecedented transparency" a signature of his government.

What is the difference, then, between the world we knew as baby
boomers and the one we see before us today? It's as if we are all now
members of a 24/7 reality TV show called *Planet Earth*, and transparency is virtually – in both senses of the word – inevitable. The
sad fate of the administration of George W. Bush was that it stead-
fastly stood firm against this historical tide, and well-nigh drowned
us all. Consider that Abu Ghraib – which we learned about when
digital images found their way on to the web – would probably not
have come to light a decade ago. From Guantanamo to Katrina to
WMDs to "Mission Accomplished," the Bush team was continually
being exposed in the hard light of a new technology that simply
didn't allow for "the shadow government" its entrenched business-
as-usual deceptions would have promulgated. Yet even as the paradigm shift was occurring all around them, they went on blithely
ignoring it.

Given that our telephones are now also digital diaries that
embrace both photography and videography as well as texting, our
first black American president may in time more tellingly be reckoned our first Blackberry president – which is to say that the new
president isn't standing firm against this centrifuge of change but
deploying and in fact pioneering it. As his campaign demonstrated,

instant communication is a made-to-order tool to actualize a vibrant democracy. And as the administration's new websites officially ratify, political transparency is now available at the press of a button.

Was there a more secretive, dissembling administration on the planet than George W. Bush's? If there was, it could only have been that of the Taliban and al-Qaida. By embracing the transparency of the new information landscape, the Obama administration in effect switches the global lights on. In this new world order, secrecy is deposed in favor of "candor," which, to quote Allen Ginsberg, "ends paranoia." As the administration proceeds on this path, recognizing that its words and deeds – subject as they are to instant review – must match up, its policies are less likely to serve as recruitment tools for terrorism, and more likely to place al-Qaida, which depends on a political ecology of secrecy, on notice.

In "Afterword: Shifting Light," I try to correlate my layman's grasp of both Einsteinian infinity and subatomic physics and then extemporize on what the larger implications might be. If we add into the equation the communication revolution, it's as if technology is beginning to approximate the generative mirroring – a form of consciousness? – at both the large and small ends of our universe.

If Vietnam was the last war America tolerated without immediate broad-based protest, the protest it eventually generated may have signaled an early warning of the hazards of combining improved information technology – at the time, television – with brutality. For many, the combination of television with Vietnam, christened "the living room war" by Michael Arlen in his *New Yorker* television columns, proved to be poisonous and intolerable.

These days, with a reporter's toolbox in every cell phone, war per se may soon be reckoned so awful as to be rendered obsolete. And as of the 2008 presidential election, America may have recaptured a leadership role in that direction.

A. S.

ARTISTS AND MODELS

INVENTING A TRADITION

IN AMERICA writers often invent their own literary traditions –
not necessarily a bad thing, given a responsive practitioner at large
among the models and monuments literature offers. Gertrude Stein
in "Composition as Explanation" asserts that each literary generation tends to favor certain verbal constructions: long sentences, short
ones, long or short paragraphs, and so on. "Paragraphs are emotional," she writes, "sentences are not."

Fifty years later, Truman Capote remarked that it was a good
idea to have a line or two of dialogue after a block of paragraphs in
order to ventilate the prose. Writers were now contending with
mass media, which made it important to be "reader friendly," a term
that came into currency near the end of the twentieth century. As a
member of the first generation of "TV babies," I remember being
drawn to the short chapters in the novels of Richard Brautigan.

These days I'm surprised by how little literary baggage my graduate students carry into class. What have they read? With one or
two exceptions per class, not a great deal, and much of it what might
be called second tier. How many, for instance, have read Norman
Mailer's *The Executioner's Song* or John Updike's *Rabbit Is Rich*?
Sometimes one student, more often none. An earlier writer such as
Willa Cather is often unfamiliar to the class as a whole.

At the same time, comic books, rechristened "graphic novels,"
have become a resource for movie adaptations. And while the larger
chain bookstores offer readers a wide selection, the books prominently displayed usually aren't classic literature but the ephemeral
popular fare of the season: the normal response, after all, of our
market-driven epoch.

In her literary essay "Mr. Bennett and Mrs. Brown," Virginia

Woolf writes that in 1910 – a year she admittedly fixes somewhat arbitrarily – a change of focus happened that would resonate throughout the century. Occurring in the same approximate time frame as Einstein's breakthrough theory of relativity, it was a shift from the bricks-and-mortar of the novels of Arnold Bennett, which take historical, geographical, architectural, and economic issues as central subject matter, to the quicksilver of human character embodied in one of Woolf's own novels – a shift from material content to consciousness, as it were.

For if Einsteinian relativity was our new description of reality, then scientifically speaking, objectively speaking, the universe was *subjective*. This claim found illustration more or less immediately in the advent of "stream of consciousness" writing brought by Woolf's generation into literary currency. Objective truth in reporting remains, of course, but with it we move momentarily back to the bricks-and-mortar model. If the judge adjourns the hearing at 3:30, it can't be said that he adjourned it at 2:00 – but what that means personally to a particular juror and/or to the defendant is the truth sought by Woolf's generation.

Truman Capote's *In Cold Blood*, appearing serially in the *New Yorker* in 1965, applied techniques he'd previously utilized as a writer of fiction to a story he found in a newspaper and then exhaustively researched. Practiced in nonfiction – as, for example, his *New Yorker* profile of Marlon Brando "The Duke in His Domain" testifies – why would the writer decide to jump tracks into his innovative hybrid, the "nonfiction novel"? One need only compare *In Cold Blood* with another mid-sixties work, "Some Dreamers of the Golden Dream," the celebrated first piece in Joan Didion's nonfiction collection *Slouching Towards Bethlehem*, to see how Capote's approach changed the literary playing field.

In the Didion piece, a complicated murder is stylistically shrink-wrapped into twenty pages dominated by an unidentified narrator who sounds like Raymond Chandler's Philip Marlowe but plays no role in the narrative. Questions are left hanging: Did the woman convicted of the murder of her husband also kill her lover's wife? Was she a textbook case from the *Diagnostic and Statistical Manual of Mental*

Disorders? A powerful style can sometimes allow one to forget the loose ends, but if attitude, even a telling one, isn't wedded to a particular figure in the story, it has the effect of disembodied "judgment."

The novelist, on the other hand, doesn't have the right to judge any character except by standing in that character's shoes – so Henry James, one of the progenitors of the shift Virginia Woolf identifies, decreed. The novelistic model wasn't judgment, that is, but empathy. As the poet Robert Duncan pointed out, Shakespeare didn't judge Iago or Lady Macbeth or Richard the Third, he invented them; and thus we leave the theater impressed powerfully by a template one might identify broadly as "reality" or "the world."

Near the end of his life – of a heart attack in 1940 at forty-four – F. Scott Fitzgerald wrote a series of essays for *Esquire* in which he takes the kind of personal inventory familiar these days in the Twelve Step recovery movement. Posthumously published in *The Crack-Up*, edited by his friend Edmund Wilson, the title essay contains this famous line: "[T]he test of a first rate intelligence is the ability to hold two opposed ideas in the mind at the same time, and still retain the ability to function." Isn't this in fact the optimal mindset of the working novelist, one equitably attuned to each character in turn, whatever that character's own opinion of another character might be?

The novelistic mind, then, comprises this paradox: It must be empathetic – otherwise how will it move into a character's shoes and circumstance? – and it must be disinterested, so that it can give life to more than one subject in the story. Echoing Fitzgerald, James Baldwin writes in his autobiographical essay "Notes of a Native Son":

> It began to seem that one would have to hold in the mind forever two ideas which seemed to be in opposition. The first idea was acceptance, the acceptance, totally without rancor, of life as it is, and men as they are: in the light of this idea, it goes without saying that injustice is a commonplace. But this did not mean that one could be complacent, for the second idea was of equal power: that one must never, in one's own life, accept these injustices as commonplace but must fight

them with all one's strength. This fight begins, however, in the heart and it now had been laid to my charge to keep my own heart free of hatred and despair.

A reading of these and other reflections suggests that the paradigm shift Woolf identifies has extraliterary implications as well: Doesn't substituting empathy (and/or acceptance in Baldwin's sense) for judgment in effect recast our idea of morality itself, moving us from a hierarchical notion of virtue to a communal sense of our shared destiny as human beings? Commenting on another novelist's call for moral fiction, John Updike remarked that what morality meant to him as a writer was simply accuracy. True to his precept, he responded to the post-9/11 world by writing a novel called *Terrorist*, in which he explored the phenomenon empathetically from the inside.

As the industrial era waned with the rise of our current informational epoch, the decade of the 1960s seemed to be a transitional flashpoint. That decade's literature, in turn, saw a deepening color palette of personal revelation combined with a larger, more demotic literary vocabulary (another echo of Shakespeare). For the writer who would invent his or her own literary tradition, the primary issue of course is to identify the most interesting and generative precursors.

If we can agree that modern narrative is composed of three primary elements –

EXPOSITION:
John walked to the corner.

REFLECTION:
Gosh, it's hot, he thought.

DIALOGUE:
"Hey, Jimmy," he said to his friend standing under the streetlight.

– then an odd truncation of the literary palette occurred in the work of central figures following the sixties. Broadly speaking, what happened is that reflection lost favor. That is, literary fiction was produced that relied heavily on exposition and dialogue – one learned of events, the bric-a-brac of circumstance, and heard how people spoke – while the inner life of a protagonist was scarcely registered. Paradoxically, the new tendency of nonfiction to utilize the techniques of fiction was reversed in the novel itself, which often favored the techniques illustrated in Joan Didion's "Some Dreamers of the Golden Dream" – which is to say with an accent on implied judgment in the absence of novelistic empathy.

A book should be good companionship, Jack Kerouac once declared. Each reader, of course, will decide what that favored mix might be, and surely that will change from day to day and week to week and, yes, epoch to epoch.

NEW AMERICAN PANTHEON

GORE VIDAL, groomed for a political career in his grandfather's footsteps, ended up our preeminent man of letters in the second half of the twentieth century, in the process surely betraying his own class and kind. Vidal trains an insider's eye on the political dumb show of our time and has given us in his collected essays, *United States* and *The Last Empire*, the most informed and readable history of our country that I know. It's a delight and conundrum that his wittily incendiary prose, penetrating to the quick the double-entry bookkeeping in Washington, is published regularly in that fat-with-ads corporate celebration *Vanity Fair*. Perhaps it's true that no one reads anymore. These essays are the clarion call of a global rather than merely national revolution, although Vidal is peerless in his coverage of our presidential ice follies. Here, in his essay "Homage to Daniel Shays," he anticipates the election of 1972, in which Richard Nixon defeated George McGovern:

> To maintain its grip on the nation, the Property Party must keep actual issues out of political debate. So far they have succeeded marvelously well. Faced with unemployment, Nixon will oppose abortion. Inflation? Marijuana is a halfway house to something worse. The bombing of North Vietnam? Well, pornographers are using the mailing lists of Cub Scouts.

The bracing chill of Vidal's vision, combined with his firsthand knowledge of the power cadres (Jacqueline Bouvier was his stepsister), and bolstered by a self-administered program of historical research, places him in the same lineage as Tom Paine, Henry Adams, and his most immediate predecessor, Edmund Wilson.

* * *

Norman Mailer was, I think, our other preeminent literary master, but while Vidal is unmatched as an essayist, Mailer's masterwork is the nonfiction novel *The Executioner's Song*, perhaps his least typical work and at the same time one that draws upon his deepest – if least advertised – powers.

Years ago, Annie Leibovitz, who had recently photographed Mailer, told me that he'd been very gracious to her, and she thought his celebrated macho persona disguised a most sensitive, thoughtful man. What is astonishing about *The Executioner's Song* is the absence in its thousand-plus pages of Mailer himself, heretofore the writer's favorite nonfiction protagonist. Instead he embodies a series of twenty-five or so recurring protagonists in a third-person narrative that novelistically adapts the speech rhythms, vocabulary, and personal slant of each character in turn. In Gary Gilmore's uncle Vern, one of the book's most memorable portraits, Mailer seems to have fortuitously discovered a psychological stand-in: a tough, grave, sweet-natured citizen who wishes deeply that his nephew would straighten up and fly right. The book is one that bears comparison with *War and Peace* or *Middlemarch*, or latterly *Doctor Zhivago*, as a panoramic orchestration of the society it depicts, and I don't know of another single work of its kind in our time that approaches it.

Mailer took his degree in engineering at Harvard, and his command of complexity has always been a hallmark, as evident in his characteristically long sentences as it is in his grasp of a daunting range of social, political, scientific, and psychological phenomena. At the same time, his study of Marilyn Monroe, for instance, while carefully atomizing the psychic makeup of an orphan, also comprises deep reserves of novelistic empathy. In *The Armies of the Night*, Mailer likewise takes the measure of Robert Lowell, with whom he shared several days during the Washington demonstration against the war in Vietnam, in what still seems the closest rendering, the finest portrait of the poet rendered from life. Indeed, Mailer is perhaps our clearest example of the ideal writer that Henry James calls for, that "someone upon whom nothing is lost."

Such a writer is so generous a benefactor that one feels a little embarrassed to confess an admittedly personal but perhaps also broadly generational reservation. One of two preeminent war novelists with his first book, *The Naked and the Dead* – the other was James Jones with *From Here to Eternity* – Mailer was a young heir of the American Empire, and like most of his literary generation, he was, it seems to me, mesmerized by power. For that generation, Jack Kennedy is the crucial figure, and anyone who saw even one of his televised press conferences knows how extraordinary he was – so witty and charismatic one might not recall the business of his political tenure. Still, to this day the only time I knew the chill of fear of nuclear annihilation was the Cuban Missile Crisis, and Kennedy is also heavily implicated in the Vietnam War.

It was another Jack of Mailer's generation, Jack Kerouac, who became one of the key models for my literary generation, and he was anomalously uninterested in power. While Kerouac and several of his friends, including Allen Ginsberg, were identified as the Beat Generation, in fact they were at most a dozen to two dozen people – nothing like a real generation. Kerouac, a French Canadian from Lowell, Massachusetts, and Mailer, a Jew from Brooklyn, were the brilliant sons of immigrant minorities who were given scholarships to the Ivy League, Mailer by Harvard and Kerouac (on a football scholarship) by Columbia, but the two responded to this social largesse in widely divergent ways. At the height of the hippie era, when I wore the long hair and bellbottoms that were the badge of my generation, I stood in midtown Manhattan one afternoon on the opposite corner from Mailer as we both waited to cross the street. Mailer was looking down and wore a preoccupied and somewhat fretful expression, whereas I was one of my generation's many impersonators of our Lord Jesus Christ. As I stood on the other side of the street waiting for the light to change, I wondered if Mailer would notice me. Eventually he looked up, saw me, lingered for a second or two, pondering, I imagine, the generational semiotics, and then looked down, quickly returning to his own preoccupations. The message conveyed was a clear one: whatever I represented was no help. Interestingly enough, Kerouac himself was also not enamored of the hippies, but as one of our key spiritual progenitors, he was rather more passionately disenchanted. Kerouac, that is, was *invested* in our generation, while Mailer, I think, might have regarded us *en masse* as a predictable defection from a standard of cool we were incapable of meeting, and of which Kennedy was the great exemplar.

In the end, I think the difference had to do with an engagement with worldly power. Intelligent older observers of the generation of the sixties kept trying – and to this day continue trying – to identify us via figures in our midst who achieved media prominence. Richard Avedon's book on the sixties is an interesting example. It's as if the World War II generation reflexively applies a hierarchical standard to what was in its essence a communal phenomenon, one first modeled for us by the Beats in their mutiny from the hierarchical terms of their own generation. The Beats, that is, put intimacy and friendship at the center of their lives. We had our stars, of course, but the communal paradigm was what was crucial and liberating. Avedon might have done better, then, to have taken his camera to Sheep's Meadow in Central Park for a free concert and photographed whomever he encountered than to photograph the usual suspects as decreed by *Time* magazine. It was the "We Generation," as it were, which still hasn't sunk in. "They got the guns," sang Jim Morrison, the son of an admiral. "But we got the numbers."

The two preeminent writers of the generation that followed Mailer, Vidal, and Kerouac, are John Updike and Philip Roth. Updike's *Rabbit Is Rich* seems to me the most exemplary American novel of my time, and the writer was also a peerless practitioner of the short story, giving us an entire lifetime in that genre from childhood through adolescence, dating rites, college, vocational quandaries, marriage, fatherhood, adultery, divorce, remarriage, and the gentle waning of powers chronicled in his last stories. The richness of his prose, a treasure trove of perceptual detail, and the largeness of his œuvre, albeit the lesser ratio of success in the novels, testify to his stature. His limit is acknowledged by Updike himself. He has stayed very close to home, giving us his intimacy with a small corner of the American middle class with an admittedly male-oriented precision that in its own terms is beyond challenge.

A political liberal who nonetheless supported the war in Vietnam,

Updike always seems slightly off his game in the cold light of day of his nonfiction. Like John Cheever, his most obvious predecessor, he is less interesting without the slight alterations of his fictional counterparts, from Rabbit Angstrom to Henry Bech. (Cheever's much-vaunted *Journals* are like stagy dress rehearsals for his stories rather than the anticipated window into his soul.) I'm unable to explain how it is that Updike invariably reviews the less-interesting book, except to call attention to the limits of my own interests. I would love to have read him on his fellow Piscean, Kerouac, of whom he became a latter-day fan after his famous early parody "On the Sidewalk," and with whom he had certain affinities. I would have liked to hear his thoughts on Mailer. Since he had populist tastes and enthusiasms – admiring, for instance, Barbra Streisand – it would have been interesting to have his thoughts on *Star Wars*. All of which is to quibble. Updike is a great and generously industrious writer.

Philip Roth seems to me best in the novella form – *Goodbye, Columbus* and *The Ghost Writer* preeminently – and I also admired his nonfiction tribute to his father, *Patrimony: A True Story*. *Portnoy's Complaint* is inspired, novel-length Borscht circuit shtick, but I wouldn't read it a second time. I recently re-read *Goodbye, Columbus* and found it bleaker than I'd remembered. As for the much-honored series of realist novels of recent years, I've been unable to read any of them – for a couple of reasons, I think.

The first is actually a question. Am I the only one who has wondered from time to time what it is, exactly, that has caused Mr. Roth to live in an apparent sustained state of rage for the better part of the last two decades? He hasn't publicly espoused the cause of the poor and exploited, written on behalf of a national health care program for all of our citizens, protested the corporate violation of our ecosystem, or called attention to the millions of American children who go hungry each day. He's a highly esteemed and highly paid literary lion of the day, and for a while was even married to the beautiful Claire Bloom. Yet each year he turns out another vituperative, not to say raging screed about the way things went for him – or rather a closely parallel fictional protagonist – in Newark or New York or Jerusalem.

The second thought may be more legitimate. Roth frequently plays fast and loose with narrative conventions, shirking them, it seems to me, at proven peril and loss in most of these outings. What is it, exactly, that he does? If we agree that virtually all good literary narrative comprises a mix of exposition, reflection, and dialogue, with individual writers emphasizing one or another of the three in a given narrative, we should also note that from time to time a very good writer will attempt to dispense with one or more elements of the mix.

I first became aware of this when I began to read Mary Robison's novel *Oh!* back in the 1980s. I'd enjoyed her book of stories *An Amateur's Guide to the Night* and looked forward to the novel. As I read the first two or three pages, I admired her exposition, which involved a helicopter hovering over people in a garden, and her always pitch-perfect dialogue. It surprised me, then, that after several pages I felt the impulse to put the book down. It was as if there was some element in it at a famine level, and I had the feeling of being almost literally jettisoned by the book.

It took several more attempts at reading those first pages of *Oh!* before I understood that the element at a famine level was that narrative equivalent of oxygen, reflection. While the characters spoke in distinct voices, and the exposition was expert, there was, in Gertrude Stein's phrase, no there there, because we were never given access to a character's interior life.

A central theme in Philip Roth's work is performance and/or dissembling. The poor young man in Newark who dates the girl from the rich part of town is trying to pass through a forbidden threshold on the strength of his good looks and intelligence, and *Goodbye, Columbus* is the beginning of an extraordinary series of literary feats in which Philip Roth stands only slightly offstage, sometimes all but visible in the wings, the handsome Jewish writer, who, having upset his people with revelations they took personally in *Portnoy's Complaint*, became the toast of New York.

Portnoy is a funny book, full of personal heat, but the character's breakneck, novel-length rant begins in a sense where it ends, which may be the problem with anger as performance. The generative premise of the book is the presence of the analyst. He never leaves the room, and we never quite see Portnoy naked of his interlocutor, whom he presumably is failing to wow even as he wows his reader very much.

In *I Married a Communist*, written thirty years later, a man tells the narrator about the life of a third man. The telling is frank and again full of heat, but the story is told virtually from beginning to end in the dialogue. In *Deception*, two adulterers talk in bed for the length of the novel. In that book, exposition, as well as reflection, is dispensed with.

Will the real Philip Roth stand up? is a question the writer, utilizing an abridged literary palette, seems to dare the reader to ask, and at the same time, that is the performance itself – the very feat for which he is awarded yet another literary prize year after year. When I returned to *Goodbye, Columbus*, an early work of gentle realism by contrast, I was surprised, as I say, by how joyless a book it is, its young protagonist too hard-nosed to enjoy the fruits of his youth. And so Philip Roth seems to have traveled through his long and distinguished literary life – in a kind of sustained discomfiture, relieved by orgasm and orgiastic vituperation. He is a good writer, a good craftsman, who has given a surcharged intensity to his work sometimes by the elimination of a key narrative element. At its best, this is what holds us, an expressionism on occasion reminiscent of the paintings of Francis Bacon or Lucian Freud. At its worst, it's as if intensity were asked to stand in for candor.

AMIRI BARAKA

WHEN I FIRST knew him, Amiri Baraka was LeRoi Jones and was married to a young Jewish woman, Hettie Cohen, and lived with her and their small children in an apartment on the Lower East Side near Astor Place. LeRoi Jones was, in those days, *the* hipster, a kind of literary Miles Davis, and while surrounded by admiring literary colleagues, most of them white, was also a pivotal social figure in bringing together the black and white artistic communities. I was nine years younger than Jones, just on my own and beginning to publish. One night at a party at his apartment, I found myself sitting on a sofa next to a young black man who looked to be around my age, twenty-one or twenty-two. We began a conversation, and I learned that he was a jazz drummer.

"Great," I said. "Are you getting any gigs these days?"

"Oh, yeah," he said.

I imagined he was approximately where I was as a writer in his career as a musician.

"No, kidding?" I said. "Lately?"

"Sure," he said. "All the time."

It turned out I was sitting next to the jazz prodigy Tony Williams, the drummer with the Miles Davis ensemble that also included the young Herbie Hancock.

The same evening, a smiling, solicitous Albert Ayler, who had a beard with a thatch of white in the middle of it said to have been caused by burns sustained in a house fire, invited me to join others in a room to hear music he'd just recorded.

I was unknown of course to either Ayler or Williams but was lucky enough to be in the home of Roi and Hettie Jones and was therefore looked upon warmly by these fellow guests.

* * *

One might speculate about the larger potentialities of such a social matrix had it endured through the sixties, but within a year, the catalyzing force at the center of the scene, Jones himself, was gone. In the early fall of 1965, he left his wife and moved to Harlem and eventually to Newark, in the process changing his name to Imamu Amiri Baraka.

For those he left behind, the move was upsetting and hard to fathom, although none of us were unsympathetic to the cause of Black Liberation, which went into high gear as the sixties began to hit its stride. Still, with the distance of almost four decades, I realize there are dimensions to what happened that I could scarcely have fathomed at the time.

Jones was just thirty when he jumped ship from the downtown scene, but uniquely among his peers, in a few short years he had realized a creative efflorescence comparable to what Allen Ginsberg had recently achieved with the publication of *Howl* and a few years later *Kaddish*.

The works I know best by Baraka are in fact the works of LeRoi Jones and were all written in whole or in part during the years of his sojourn in Lower Manhattan. There are the poetry volumes, *Preface to a Twenty Volume Suicide Note* and *The Dead Lecturer*, the novel *The System of Dante's Hell*, the book of stories *Tales*, the collection of essays *Home*, and his music history *Blues People*. On top of these, in a quantum leap that delivered him into mainstream fame, came the play *Dutchman*, at the Cherry Lane Theater, produced by Wilder and Barr, the team that had brought on Edward Albee a few years earlier.

During the brief period in which he declared his disaffection with his milieu, Jones appeared on a panel with Larry Rivers, who had done sets for one of his plays, and told him that he considered their friendship expendable and reportedly settled a dispute with Dwight Macdonald, the tall, reedy anarcho-pacifist patriarch, by punching him.

When I saw *Dutchman*, it was clear to me that he had effectively changed the game we had been playing up to that point, doing something bigger and bolder than we were accustomed to seeing from one of our own.

At the 2002 Pan-African Film Festival in Los Angeles, where he received the Lifetime Achievement Award, Baraka commented that after the play opened and he read the reviews, he realized, "They were going to make this boy famous." When the movie of the play, made during the sixties, was shown at the festival, it struck me that in its own terms, the play might have been another presentiment of Jones's move.

Conceived as a long subway ride, *Dutchman* is an extended *pas de deux* between a young straight-arrow black man, Clay, dressed in a suit and tie, and a sexually predatory white woman who preys on successive incarnations of Clay's type.

Beautifully performed by the young Shirley Knight and Al Freeman Jr., the film reverses the sexual stereotype of the day (and ours): the delicate white girl assaulting the black man, the erstwhile standard bearer of sexual prowess and danger. For the better part of the ride, a politely bemused Clay endures an increasingly vicious, albeit brazenly sexual onslaught from the nameless white female, and then, when he finally erupts in anger and scorn to claim an identity that in his white collar uniform he has heretofore suppressed, she pulls a knife out of her purse and murders him.

The ramifications here seem virtually endless, especially if one assumes that LeRoi Jones is both of his creations. The same could be said of the two characters of Albee's breakthrough play *The Zoo Story*, who might be regarded as different sides of the same nature. On the one hand, we have Peter, who seems to have come to terms rather too perfectly with his world and time; and on the other Jerry, a charismatic artist maudit who has nothing at all to show for his game. Then, in the play's last turns, comes an act of violence in which the different sides these two represent might be said to symbolically merge. Jerry taunts and teases Peter to his feet and into reluctant, halfhearted combat – but as it turns out, it's more as if he's engaging him as an unwitting collaborator in his suicide. In the play's final moments, Jerry thrusts his own switchblade into Peter's hands and then impales himself on the knife. If one looks upon *The Zoo Story* as a parable, it's as if the artist figure makes the decision to merge his anarchic (and creative) energies with the love of formal routine that makes his interlocutor, however dull, the successful citizen, and survivor, that he is. Aesthetically speaking, the enactment of this parable would appear to be validated in being followed closely by Albee's three-act masterwork, *Who's Afraid of Virginia Woolf?*

In *Dutchman*, on the other hand, something entirely different is enacted. Clay, as he is called, at first seems, like his counterpart Peter in *The Zoo Story*, rather too perfectly molded to society's order, a fledgling black bourgeois. An innocent riding the subway, he is engaged and outrageously challenged by a white Medusa figure who seems to take a different shape with each utterance. When Clay finally erupts against her violent presumption, and mocks her attempt to impersonate the physical freedom identified with his race, she murders him, without protest from the other passengers on board.

The significant decision of the play, then – the equivalent of Jerry's decision in *The Zoo Story* to immolate himself – is Clay's decision, at last, to declare his own deeper racial identity. When he does this, he is murdered, evidently with impunity. The final image of *Dutchman* is the white female stalking a fresh-faced, unsuspecting new incarnation of Clay.

What we witness, then, is the ritual murder of a black man by a serial killer of the white race who is female. Make of it what you will, the play ends without the thinnest hope of redemption. Either Clay sticks to his disguise or he isn't long for this world, and his tormentor isn't going to make it easy for him to ride along in his life. LeRoi Jones, author of the play and the darling of the white downtown literary world, was soon to leave the scene – with a famous name that he simultaneously changed.

"I was a wild boy," Baraka said during an interview that preceded the award ceremony. "But when you become – adult," he said, "you have to take responsibility." In the end, the difference between the two plays may be that Albee wrote an aesthetic parable and Jones a political one.

Baraka was obviously an adored hero of the black community assembled to honor him at the Magic Johnson Theater complex in Leimert Park. A great speaker, he exhorted the community to organize its $400 billion buying power to effect the changes it sought, and went on, after the presentation, to read two long poems, one of which was "Somebody Blew Up America," the 9/11 poem he later read at his inauguration as poet laureate of New Jersey, setting off a firestorm of outrage.

Both poems were exhortations, excoriating the global corporate hegemony. Here was this dapper, graying eminence, with a hint of a stoop in his shoulders now – whereas in his youth, it seemed a hipster's slight forward tip of his carriage – and he read with a loud, declarative musical scorn, a take-no-prisoners anthem to his people and against a power structure that made them suffer, along with other nonwhite races across the planet.

In our briefly shared youth, Baraka had been kind to me, supportive of my own fledgling efforts.

"It's good to see you flexing your muscles," he told me one night at a Greenwich Village bar after I'd sent him an issue of the little magazine I'd started. It was a fraternal, almost familial remark from a time that wasn't to endure for long, a moment of innocence in which we both might have imagined we would see each other routinely over the years.

A nagging question regarding this gifted, protean writer is the apparently stunted achievement of the years that followed his initial surge as LeRoi Jones. On the one hand, it could be argued that Allen Ginsberg, who never matched the power of his two major poems, nevertheless became an even more important figure as he grew older. One remembers the shocking news photograph of Baraka recently repatriated to Newark, where he'd grown up, with his head bleeding after an encounter with the police. There was the Les Crane television talk show – perhaps the most accurate media representation of the sixties as it occurred – during which Baraka refused to directly answer Crane's questions but used each one as an opportunity to exhort the black community with Marxist–Leninist analysis/agitprop. I remember too his appearance during the 1970s at New College in Berkeley in an auditorium flanked by bodyguards stationed on either side of the hall. He addressed the largely white left-liberal crowd with the repeated injunction to achieve a "dictatorship of the proletariat," a phrase from an old-style Marxist handbook.

I found myself frustrated by Baraka's New College performance because he seemed to embrace Marxism virtually by number. For all his espousal of his African heritage, it was as if he was taking his cues from Jean-Paul Sartre, an old-line European Stalinist. When I raised my hand and asked him what he thought of Boris Pasternak, he answered that he was more interested in the more revolutionary Mayakovsky – an odd choice, I thought, since the poet had committed suicide during Stalin's terrorist reign, which he had first tried to embrace as a stalwart.

"If you say something's wrong, but you're not sure what it is – they call that art," Baraka paraphrased Sartre at the film festival. "But if you say something's wrong, and you *know* who's fault it is, that's just social protest."

Even given the tempering of the intervening years – he spoke admiringly of Martin Luther King Jr., for instance, as he wouldn't have during the sixties – there was still an edge of violence about Baraka's directives, an "us-and-them" template that may still be energizing for the larger black community but doesn't seem to work as a generative resource for the artist in process. It is this understanding, perhaps, that stands behind the sly, love-you-madly posturing of Duke Ellington or the various witty, evasive personas of Lester Young and Thelonious Monk, among other black artists.

While many in white America feel anger and alienation at being held in a kind of social and economic lockdown by the transnational global hegemony, the situation is far worse for many in the American black community. And Baraka speaks to that difference, discarding aesthetic finer points to address a well-nigh lifelong sociopolitical emergency. And so Allen Ginsberg also seemed to see it, although he wouldn't demonize his opposition.

"America, I am putting my queer shoulder to the wheel," he wrote at the beginning of his career. LeRoi Jones was surely among those who heard him at the time, and he was to do likewise, albeit that his was a black shoulder. As he wrote at the beginning of his career with the force of language and perception that he still commands:

. . . Loud spics kill each other, and will not

make the simple trip to Tiffany's. Will not smash their
    stainless
heads, against the simpler effrontery of so callous a code
    as gain.

At the Pan-African Film Festival he called for a coalition across the
lines of the vast nonwhite majority on the planet, with an acknowledgment of sympathetic whites *en passant*, and addressed the young
brothers of his own race. "We need your force," he said. "Go on, be
bad. Just don't be stupid."

    With the advent of Barack Obama, one wonders what his thoughts
are now.

FIELDING DAWSON
1930–2002

MY FIRST ENCOUNTER with Fielding Dawson happened on an early evening during the spring of 1964 in New York City. Robert Creeley, with whom I'd been corresponding, had recommended that I call on Dawson, and I'd telephoned and arranged to meet him at the end of his workday at Bon Marché, a furniture store on Third Avenue in midtown where he was employed as a salesman. By this time, also on Creeley's recommendation, I'd read the several stories by Dawson in LeRoi Jones's anthology *The Moderns*, and this work had made a strong impression on me.

One of the stories was about a man and a woman in the Midwest; it told of their love affair in a very different climate and geography than one knew in New York – a small town with quiet sidewalks where, just around the corner, one might glimpse a stretch of prairie miles. The woman, named Valley, was both a person and a kind of magnetic force field, and the man went by the wonderful name of Webster Groves, which I later learned was a town in Dawson's Midwestern environs. There was a spaciousness and grandeur to the story, and I was expecting to encounter a quiet, dignified man who might be difficult to get to know.

Instead, Fee Dawson emerged from the back of the store, a slightly plump six-footer with a disarming smile and a kind, solicitous manner.

"Well, how are *you*?" he said, and eyed me merrily.

I was twenty years old, and Fielding was thirty-three, married at the time to a young woman named Barbara, only a year or two older than I.

* * *

Of all the writers I've known, Fee Dawson was the most in love with the idea of being a writer – a writer in New York City, I should say. The writers that endure in that red-hot cauldron are rather few and far between, when you think about it. Manhattan has been, perhaps, a poet's city, but seldom the residence of a creative prose writer after a year or two. But the young man I saw in the bright environs of Bon Marché that evening was already devoutly wedded to a unique New York literary destiny, come what may.

We went out to a local bar, had dinner and several beers, and talked like fast friends. Fielding was writing stories set in Manhattan now, often at his day job, and these stories were very different from those that took place in his earlier landscape. The long vistas had been replaced by an almost claustrophobic psychological expressionism. He would catch – field? – psychological and/or sexual nuances between coworkers or co-denizens of a Manhattan bar or at a party with a fierce, accelerated accuracy that might also include, dream-like, a psychological freeze-frame.

The man I'd been expecting – a grave, slow-spoken citizen of the prairie – wasn't anyone you'd be likely to find in Dawson. Instead he was hale, hearty, bluff, warm, somewhat bullying in a friendly way, a little unsure of himself, slightly feminine within his cocksure persona – like a sort of living Willem de Kooning "Man" painting, had the painter traded genders for his masterpiece.

Barbara, his wife, was pretty, rather voluptuous, and more or less surrendered the floor to Fee in our discussions.

During the time I knew him, Dawson lived in the same loft off Union Square. It was a big cavernous place, and it seemed more or less a makeshift encampment – bed, table to eat at, and, importantly, work-desk where Fee did his writing. He also made paintings and collages, but it didn't feel like a painter's loft. It was a writer's place. Curiously, I don't recall a library, although Fee would be taken with literary enthusiasms – Raymond Chandler, Ross Macdonald, perhaps even John D. MacDonald, all in one fell swoop. It was a writer's reading, that is, in which he would be following out some common thread he found in each.

After I got to know him, Fee would invite me to meet him at the

Cedar Tavern for beers, and in my case this meant, simply, getting drunk. I was a somewhat repressed post-adolescent, and for a while, at least, this seemed a salutary procedure. I didn't know many people very well, that is, and such an evening promised an emotional opening, this sharing with another, elder writer – although Fee never played seniority very hard. I think he simply enjoyed having company as he drank, and he would fix one with his amused urgency, and his perennial enthusiasm – we were writers in New York, don't forget – and I found this engaging and even endearing.

Fee was most likely clinically an alcoholic – much as, say, Bukowski was. On that score, Bukowski came up with a formulaic short story – often involving an unhappy female companion – and wrote this story a hundred times or more.

Similarly, Fee's stories involved incidents along the daily round of his Manhattan world from loft to bar to – when he was working – job, and the denizens of that circuit. Often a story involved the protagonist enduring a psychological jolt of some sort, and then, perhaps, getting his recompense. While their quality could vary, the stories hold you with their narrative ease and accuracy. They have the pressure of a real life.

We honor writers of this ilk, I think, whatever the limits of their work, because they do speak of actual life, while so many others today seem to be merely living literary careers.

Personally, after a year or two, I was to grow impatient with Fielding's routine. The young may model a particular nervous system, try it on for size for a while, looking for a natural alignment, and when it doesn't pan out, doesn't prove to be a good fit, can be abrupt in moving on.

Or so it seemed to go with Dawson and me. Still, I went on reading him, taking pleasure in his work. In the end, his writing comprises a fluent adventure of mind, body, and spirit that remains, I think, a valuable literary resource, an ongoing legacy. And even when I no longer looked him up when I was in New York, I was aware he was there, just a phone call away, ever engaged in his enterprise, making his stories, making his paintings and drawings, living his life. He was an original.

THE BUKOWSKI CROWN

WHEN THE POET-CRITIC Dana Gioia wrote recently in the *New York Times* that "Los Angeles is perhaps the only great city in the world that has not yet produced a great poet," there was an immediate public outcry, most of it pointing reproachfully in the direction of the late Charles Bukowski. The French poet-polymath Jean Cocteau liked to speak of the poetry of film, the poetry of dance, the poetry of song, et al., and, had he been on hand and so inclined, would have no doubt entered the fray invoking a multitude of other names, beginning perhaps with Charles Chaplin and including such diverse figures as Edward Weston, John Cassavetes, Marvin Gaye, Joni Mitchell, Jim Morrison, and The Eagles. But staying more strictly within the given parameters, the protest has focused on Bukowski, and anyone who writes in Los Angeles can take heart from such public ardor in the name of literature. Still, there seems to me both more and less in this choice of our great man than has so far been discussed.

Charles Bukowski had endearing qualities. In a feminist age, he's unapologetically chauvinist, which makes him a sort of cockeyed hero, keeping the dark side of the picture in view. He was also in love with being a writer: one who after years of low-paying jobs to keep him in booze with a roof over his head, got rich and famous for his stories, poems, and novels about being a half-looped, rough-and-ready romantic. The laugh's on everybody who bugged him in the first place, who are legion. Bukowski isn't generous in his assessments of others, or very interested anyhow. His novel *Hollywood*, based on the making of the movie *Barfly*, directed by Barbet Schroeder and starring Mickey Rourke and Faye Dunaway, contains only one fully drawn character, himself. Everybody else makes what might be called cameo homages.

But more problematic to me is a younger generation, including famous actors like Sean Penn, Mickey Rourke, and Michael Madsen, who long ago awarded Bukowski a literary crown and laurel wreath. At the risk of ticking off one or more of these rumble-prone eminences, I need to protest. I know he's easy and enjoyable reading, my brothers, and I don't scoff at that, but so are Salinger, Hemingway, and, well, Albert Camus – to name only three – and contrary to his own notions, Buk doesn't make it into their company. He's like a musician who can only play two or three tunes. The ending of the most popular one has an outraged blonde yelling at the top of the stairs that, nine times out of ten, Henry Chinaski, Bukowski's stand in, just fell down.

Henry James's measure for literature was the amount of "felt life" it contained. A great part of Bukowski's value is that he brings into view a darker world than is generally permissible in mainstream American writing. William Burroughs's first novel, *Junkie*, wasn't considered publishable after the Second World War, although it was impeccably written – not because its subject was criminal lowlife and junkies in Manhattan, but because the narrator never spoke of his own or anyone else's moral rehabilitation. It was originally published in the early fifties as one side of an Ace "double giant" mass paperback under Burroughs's pseudonym William Lee.

Bukowski's work has similarities with *Junkie*, notwithstanding that it's full of romance about being a writer, come hell or high water, as his exemplar John Fante's work is. Fante in fact may be the only writer whom Bukowski admires unreservedly.

I don't want to diminish a considerable achievement. Bukowski has given writing and reading to a large public that might otherwise shine it, as they used to say. At the same time, one might hope that such an act would provide an entrée into the larger house of literature. What seems to happen instead is that getting to the front room where Bukowski presides doesn't spur many readers to move farther inside.

Part of the problem may be traceable to the writer's general disdain for his literary peers and elders. In *Hollywood*, he remarks that F. Scott Fitzgerald's heart attack at forty-four in Los Angeles was the result of his going on the wagon. Presumably if Bukowski had been there, he could have saved the author of *The Great Gatsby* and *Tender Is the Night* by pouring him another drink. On the other hand, he might have written him off by then as a has-been and not bothered.

The critic Philip Rahv divided American literature into two camps: the pale faces and the red skins, those who worked away in their studies and the men and women who went out into the wide world for extensive sojourns and *then* wrote it down. Part of the appeal of a writer like Raymond Carver, for example, is that he did both. A consummate craftsman, he also got entangled in a problematic and partly tortuous life journey that many on their own roads could identify with personally. Thus Carver can give solace to fellow sojourners, providing the "good companionship" that Kerouac decreed was the best that literature has to offer.

For all his let-it-rip persona, Bukowski, in the end, is a very practiced literary *stylist* with a product that never seems to spur him on to another threshold. This may or may not have something to do with alcoholism. In the Twelve Step program of Alcoholics Anonymous, they say that the addict or alcoholic remains the emotional age he was when his addiction took hold and advances from that age only when he goes into recovery. Bukowski appears not to have been interested in recovery, and by this measure presumably remained emotionally the same age throughout his career. What you encounter in his stories is a man who is palpably thrilled to be able to write about being a drunk: that is, to be able to be a practicing drunk and a practicing writer at the same time. It's a macho turn of, I suppose, unexpected originality.

What about that, then? What about risking getting in a car wreck or setting fire to the bed or getting beaten up badly because one got loaded one time too many? At bottom, that is the drama of the Bukowski story. "The only thing that matters is how you walk through the fire," he wrote and somebody quoted on a big billboard on Olympic Boulevard recently.

The crux of it, I think, has to do with keeping one's humanity and vulnerability in play after signing off on the give-and-take of an ongoing relationship, for instance, or any other equivalent surrender to the other. In effect, the macho hero moves us in his willingness to face death *in lieu of* a letting go in tamer circumstances: love, friendship, study, or any other less physically threatening form of surrender.

In his book *A Separate Reality* about the Yaqui Indian *brujo* Don Juan, Carlos Castaneda, a writer very much in the Hemingway lineage, speaks of death "as an advisor." And surely awareness of death quickens one's sense of vulnerability, in lieu of more domestic concerns that seem to play on the self to the same effect: mate, children, parents, social and political commitments, etc.

For a man of Bukowski's generation, one problem with being a writer, a poet into the bargain, was that such a calling could cast doubt over one's manhood. The finer feelings can get a man into trouble in our day of corporate gunslingers, let alone the earlier one of the John Wayne/Ernest Hemingway male prototype that was Bukowski's immediate inheritance. In his *Paris Review* interview, James Jones, who wrote the epic World War II novel *From Here to Eternity*, and thus became one of two primary inheritors of the Hemingway mantle in his generation (the other being Norman Mailer), remarks that in a period in which men are challenged to fight to prove their masculinity, not fighting could be a sign of greater courage.

Jones's remark opens a window into the deeper levels of male consciousness in our time. On the other hand, here is our old friend Bukowski/Chinaski shot to pieces again after his latest roisterous romantic encounter. He doesn't take himself too seriously, anyway, with the exception of getting in a dig now and then at some presumed competition in the room. Bukowski is fine, I want to say. But can he really be a model of the first-rank artist? Or isn't he, rather, an easy interlude – and thank God for them – before you move on to something actually great. *Middlemarch*, say. Or *Fathers and Sons*. Or, closer to our own time, *Doctor Zhivago*. Or Ralph Ellison's *Invisible Man*.

Getting wrecked may be one way to access a larger color palette of self than might otherwise be available to a man of Bukowski's time and temper. But it's not going to be complicated, and it isn't likely that he's going to be able to see or write more than one character in the round. Finally, that's what the limit is: It all keeps coming back to the rugged, beleaguered one, all alone in his room with a bottle and his typewriter.

POETS OF THE REALM

ALMOST A DECADE AGO I was interviewed by Michael Silverblatt on his radio show *Bookworm.* I'd edited Ted Berrigan's posthumous *Selected Poems,* and the show was an opportunity to talk about Ted and his work and to publicize the book. In the middle of the interview, Silverblatt surprised me by remarking that Ted and I and a number of other poets, including Ron Padgett and Tom Clark, represented a second generation of the New York School but that we hadn't managed to live up to the achievement of the first generation: Frank O'Hara, John Ashbery, Kenneth Koch, and James Schuyler.

"Isn't the next generation supposed to improve on its predecessors?" Silverblatt mused rhetorically.

I held back on several possible responses and tried to make a case for the fact that Tom Clark, for example, was the author of a far larger œuvre than any member of the first generation and had written in a greater variety of genres. Perhaps temporizing, Silverblatt went on to say that the difference was that we hadn't had to measure ourselves against a masterpiece like *The Waste Land* and therefore wrote more modestly.

We had measured ourselves against Ginsberg's *Howl* and *Kaddish,* among other works. And Ted's book-length poem *The Sonnets* is, in its way, an exhilarating successor. What is more true of our generation is that we didn't play by the rules of the literary establishment. We came of age during the sixties and paid a commensurate price in censure and revisionism for that. The first generation of "TV babies," raised during the post–World War II economic boom, we were less grateful for our parents' sacrifices than we might have been, while at the same time being natural denizens of a newly electrified culture.

I might have added that I myself was only nominally a New York School poet. My first allegiance had been to the Black Mountain poets, to Robert Creeley, Denise Levertov, Robert Duncan, Charles Olson, and Edward Dorn, and to a number of others as well. Indeed there was a time when these poets meant everything to me, when they embodied the possibility of the kind of life I wanted for myself.

All are gone now, and I'm struck by the shape of their various careers in long view. Charles Olson and Robert Duncan seem to me to be major American poets, great and generative figures as much today as they were during the sixties. Denise Levertov is a personal favorite though her range is more modest. Robert Creeley and Edward Dorn, on the other hand, wonderful poets in youth, both seem to have lost their way in midlife.

Robert Creeley's early work, including poems, stories, essays, and perhaps crowned by his novel *The Island*, published when he was in his mid-thirties, holds the promise of a major American literary figure. Edward Dorn, also a practitioner of all these genres, seemed to many of us a figure of comparable promise with perhaps a broader vision of the American sociopolitical as well as ecological landscape. Dorn, only three years younger than Creeley, had been a student at Black Mountain College during the years when Creeley taught there.

At twenty, having gotten an assignment from Henry Rago at *Poetry* to review *The Island*, I dared to write to Creeley in New Mexico from New York and was rewarded beyond expectation with a long and interesting letter about his sources as a writer. As we exchanged several more letters, I was moving around in search of an apartment and remember writing him from a hotel in Brooklyn Heights where I stayed only a night or two. Those were heady days. For me, corresponding with Creeley was what I imagined it might have been like for a young political aspirant to correspond with then-President Kennedy.

Here is a favorite poem from Creeley's first mainstream collection, *For Love*:

THE END

When I know what people think of me
I am plunged into my loneliness. The grey

hat bought earlier sickens.
I have no purpose no longer distinguishable.

A feeling like being choked
enters my throat.

There is a wonderful poker-faced humor to this bleak poem, signaled in the title and also in the clotted syntax of the fourth line. It's so vividly an emotional thing and at the same time a made thing, a fact of words that delivers its message with the artful-artlessness of a young master of what would come to be known as the Black Mountain School. Looking through the book the other night, I was struck by how often Creeley uses a title as a distancing device, while the poem itself may be entirely enveloped in the dilemma it presents.

What distinguishes these early poems is the personal detail, the signature of a more-than-literary life. Robert Bly pointed out that the energy and specificity of these poems is diluted in later volumes, by which time the poet, as so many have done to survive, had become a tenured professor. The recent biography by Ekbert Faas notes that during the sixties, Allen Ginsberg told Creeley that he didn't necessarily have to write "good" poems, advice he seemed to take almost literally. What followed was the book called *Pieces*, a book-length sequence in which very short notations are arranged down the pages with a kind of blithe insouciance, as if to say, I'm a poet and therefore this is poetry. This is the way Creeley would often henceforth write. Being a technical master, given a particular circumstance or assignment, he would on occasion write a fine poem or essay. But the early work is another order of achievement, full to bursting with "felt life," Henry James's measure for literature.

Edward Dorn once said to me regarding Creeley that his handicap – a missing eye since a childhood accident, over which Creeley wore no patch – added something to his mystique, something perhaps comparable in its effect to Byron's club foot. In fact, Dorn himself was the best-looking white-man poet of his day, a tall, angular figure with a handsome face akin to the textbook renderings of Andrew Jackson. My first encounter with him occurred in the summer of 1964, when my friend Jim Brodey and I visited LeRoi Jones in

Buffalo, where he and his family were sharing a house with Dorn and his family, both poets teaching in the summer session at the state university there.

Dorn, celebrated among his peers and an admired elder of Jim's and my generation, proved to be an elusive figure, darting in and out of the living room once or twice as Jones generously played host to the two young poets. In part spurred by his unavailability, I audited one of Dorn's classes.

I don't think I could have told you what it was about five minutes after it ended, although the subject included Melville, but Dorn was a marvel to see and hear. Seated at his desk at the front of the class, he didn't engage in dialogue with students. At the same time, it was somehow casual and unassuming. He simply spoke, and the combination of his voice and his diction was spellbinding. He had a special way with vowels, evident in his poetry; and his wonderfully even pitch and intonation, coupled with word choices seemingly conjured out of the moment, made up a kind of spoken music. Here is the title poem of Dorn's collection *The Newly Fallen*, which had appeared several years earlier:

IF IT SHOULD EVER COME

And we are all there together
Time will wave as willows do
And adios will be truly, yes,

laughing at what is forgotten

and talking of what's new
admiring the roses you brought.
How sad.

You didn't know you were at the end
thought it was your bright pear
the earth, yes
another affair to have been kept
and gazed back on

> when you had slept
> to have been stored
> as a squirrel will a nut, and half
> forgotten,
> there were so many, many
> from the newly fallen.

The music in these words, a kind of dancing melancholy, seems to me the signature of Dorn's greatest work. He was raised by Illinois farm people without the advantages of Harvard-trained peers like Creeley save his gift and the effort with which he cultivated and refined it. Dorn's early, long-lined poems "Geranium" and "The Air of June Sings" deserve a place among the permanent American poems, I think, being the closest I know in our literature to the musical complexity and felicity of the Elizabethans.

What happened? Over the years, the voice gradually turned into a hipster's cutting, sarcastic instrument, often so elliptical as to be incomprehensible. Somehow the shading and suffering in his early work was foregone. This happened gradually, and he never succumbed to the willfulness one finds in middle and later Creeley. He remained a searching and interesting poet, but he no longer moved one as he had. Like virtually everybody who experienced the sixties firsthand, Dorn experimented with drugs, and one can imagine that so finely tuned a verbal musician might have been more affected by them than others who had never made such music.

Denise Levertov's poetry engaged me from high school, seeming to find principles in observed nature that applied to the human sphere. In an early poem, "Overland to the Islands," the object of her reflection is a dog:

> Under his feet
> rocks and mud, his imagination, sniffing,
> engaged in its perceptions – dancing
> edgeways, there's nothing
> the dog disdains on his way,
> nevertheless he

keeps moving, changing
pace and approach but
not direction – 'every step an arrival.'

I submitted poems to her at the *Nation* when she was the poetry
editor there, and while she never took a poem, she replied graciously
to each submission and invited me to her Manhattan apartment for
a gathering of young poets where we sat in a circle and read our
poems. For me she was a poet heroine, a lovely woman unbridled by
the prefeminist world in which she lived. I never got to know her
and when the sixties went into gear lost touch with her entirely, but
I continued to take heart from her work, even when its explicitly
political stance caused a semipublic rift with Robert Duncan.

Reading her *Selected Poems* these days, I find in it qualities I
didn't note much at the time, although I imagine they impressed me.
Levertov writes unmistakably as a woman. With a kind of feminine
propriety, she speaks directly and often movingly of her sexuality, her
marriage with the novelist Mitchell Goodman, their eventual divorce,
and her years alone. It's hard to say what it is, exactly, that moves one
in a poet. Robert Duncan, for example, a poet I admire as much as any
I know, exhilarates and inspires but doesn't move one as Levertov
does, perhaps because the large culture that Duncan brings to the
page gives one the sense that he is less alone in the world.

Of all the poets I've known, Duncan seemed to me the most at home
in the role. To be at home in oneself as an artist in America is, I think,
the rarest kind of achievement. In his essay "The Homosexual in
Society," which appeared in Dwight Macdonald's magazine *politics*
when Duncan was in his mid-twenties, he publicly declared himself
a gay man. It was 1944. It may be that his involvement with language-
as-vocation spurred him to such thresholds. Like Allen Ginsberg, he
was a person who seemed to have opened most of the doors in himself, and in Duncan this yielded a vivacious ease. One sees in retro-
spect that he was a living master.

Duncan was a nonstop monologist, but he wasn't self-absorbed
in the way of other monologists. Rather, speech, either written or
spoken, was for him a medium of access to the largest field of pos-

sibilities. He wrote once that he made poetry the way other men made love or went to war, to exercise his faculties at large. He isn't always an easy poet, but his music is evident even if his exact meaning can be elusive. In the end it may be that the music in the words is the most exact meaning poetry affords. I discovered a signed copy of *The Opening of the Field* in a San Diego bookstore years ago in which Duncan had quoted his own lines:

> "so that he sees and sings
> central threnodies, as if a life had
> but one joyous thread. . ."

> Robert Duncan
>   at home, October 9, 1976

The "at home" seems telling, as with his longtime partner, the painter Jess Collins, Duncan achieved a domestic equilibrium from which his poetry flowed like Bach concerti.

I never met Charles Olson, but reading *The Maximus Poems* (around the time I was corresponding with Creeley) was a powerful and informing experience that has lasted a lifetime:

> the mind, that worker on what is

> an American
> is a complex
> of occasions

> polis
> is
> eyes

> words words words, all over everything

> cause is not
> the equal of

the error of

act

I probably have some of the line breaks wrong, but these lines became personal touchstones. In the seventies, I read and reviewed for the *Nation* his marvelous memoir of his father, *The Post Office*, which was written early in his writing career and has a different, quieter, more personal tone than his later poetry. *Call Me Ishmael*, his study of *Moby Dick*, was a great influence on both the style and substance of my book *Genesis Angels: The Saga of Lew Welch and the Beat Generation*. In 1965 I solicited work from him in Gloucester for my little magazine, *Lines*, and he graciously sent me a Maximus poem.

One night that year in my New York studio apartment, in an apocalyptic mood known to infect twenty-one-year-old beginning writers, I addressed the great man in a letter. Creeley and Olson had been the chief purveyors of the technical side of the Black Mountain School of poetry, Creeley with his much-quoted maxim, "Form is never more than an extension of content"; and Olson with his definitive essay "Projective Verse." In the meantime, however, in editing *Lines*, I'd opened myself up to a range of other traditions and personalities, including Ted Berrigan's liberating version of the New York School and Ian Hamilton Finlay's concrete poetry. "Form *is* content!" I remember exclaiming in the letter to Olson. At that moment it was no doubt the whole truth as I knew it, just then breaking into my minimal period of one-word poems, etc. In the year or so interim since I'd corresponded with Creeley, I'd also evidently gotten bolder with my elders and betters.

I didn't hear from Olson and grew to regret my own letter as an aberration that most likely had offended him. About six months after I'd mailed the letter, out of the blue, I received a postcard – the post office variety with no picture on it – boldly addressed to me in pencil. "My dear Saroyan," Olson wrote, "I couldn't figure out exactly why you were addressing *me*." This laser-like reading of the situation reduced me to laughter and even greater (enduring) admiration.

A FINE ROMANCE

THE GENERATION THAT came to light in American poetry after the
Second World War differed from the one that immediately preceded
it – the generation of Robert Lowell, Randall Jarrell, John Berryman,
et al. – by taking its aesthetic bearings primarily from Ezra Pound
and William Carlos Williams rather than from T. S. Eliot. A stateside
retinue of Eliot-influenced poet-critics, comprising the movement
known as the New Criticism, looked to the seventeenth-century meta-
physical poets for models and emphasized levels of meaning that
were to be teased out of a text, as it were, with scalpel and forceps.

Partly in response to this chilly, daunting literary climate, alle-
giances were forged, often across significant geographical distance,
among aspiring poets in their early twenties at the end of the war.
These informal confederations included the first generation of the
New York School (Frank O'Hara, John Ashbery, James Schuyler,
Kenneth Koch), the Beat Generation (Ginsberg, Kerouac, Gregory
Corso) and the Black Mountain School that included Charles Olson,
Robert Creeley, Robert Duncan, and Denise Levertov. This latter
group was the most engaged by aesthetic questions and dynamics,
and none more so than Robert Duncan, who grew into a kind of
venerable Magus figure of the new American poetry and was the
initiator of this voluminous and unique correspondence.*

A foster child raised in a Theosophist household in Bakersfield,
Duncan was handsome, albeit cross-eyed, and homosexual – and
he possessed the most exacting and musical ear of all his peers.
While given to hermetic scholarly studies ("I'm reading too much!"

---

* *The Letters of Robert Duncan and Denise Levertov.* Edited by Robert J.
Bertholf and Albert Gelpi. Stanford University Press: Stanford, California. 2004.
857 pp.

he writes to Levertov at one point), he could also be charmingly gregarious.

In an issue of the little magazine *Origin*, the early house organ of the Black Mountain poets edited by Cid Corman out of Boston, Duncan first came across a poem by Levertov that he very much admired and wrote her a poem/letter in response.

Levertov, the beautiful English-bred and homeschooled daughter of a Jewish father and a Welsh mother, at first didn't know what to make of the poem, entitled "An A Muse Ment" and thought it might be a putdown. When this misunderstanding was cleared up, the two fell headlong into epistolary love.

Their correspondence comprises 479 letters and begins in 1953. After the sixties, it tapers off sharply – the two clashed over their responses to the Vietnam War – but for the better part of two decades, the reader is privy to the day-to-day lives – with their full complement of brights and darks – of two major figures of twentieth-century American poetry.

While the successive generations of Eliot-influenced poets moved seamlessly into tenured academia, the newer voices celebrated in Donald M. Allen's benchmark anthology *The New American Poetry* moved hardly at all in that direction. Duncan and Levertov live much of their youth – Duncan with his partner the painter Jess Collins, Levertov married to the American novelist and social activist Mitchell Goodman – as Laurentian adventurers at large in the world. In the early letters especially, there are intimately telling glimpses of such figures as Kenneth Rexroth, Kenneth Patchen, H.D. and her patroness Bryher, Allen Ginsberg, and Robert and Ann Creeley in Majorca, where both Duncan and the Goodmans lived at separate times early on.

The appearance of Allen Ginsberg's *Howl* rocks the poetry world of Duncan and Levertov's day much as Eliot's *The Waste Land* rocked it in the 1920s. Levertov, often an astute critic, writes to Duncan from Guadalajara in October 1956:

We received *Howl* a few days ago. It seems to us very impressive. . . It has the strength & truth of a man's real voice – nothing put-up, contrived, smoothed to please – yet it has variety within itself – it's not a strident complaint – there's a non-sugary sweetness (honey) in a line like "The kindly search for growth, the gracious desire to exist of the flowers. . ." akin to Whitman's "Tall sunflower creaking on its stalk."

Both poets have a flair for rendering the daily domestic round, sometimes at their own comic expense. Levertov, who hadn't ridden a bike in a long time and recalls a near-disaster when her brakes gave out as she rode into a square in the South of France, writes to Duncan from Oaxaca in 1957 that she's a little wary of taking up a bike again with her young son, Nikolai. In her next letter, she reports:

> I had a most exhilarating ride with Nik, who was beautifully calm on *his* machine – but sure enough, 2 blocks from home, somewhat rattled by a dog that made some pretence to rush out & bark at my ankles, albeit half-heartedly, I ran straight into a guy playing ball in the street (not a kid, either), & thereafter reclined in an Etruscan position under my bike berating him in English as "Idiot" and "Peahead!" Two businessmen picked me up & dusted me & checked the health of the wheels. I said indignantly, "And the oaf didn't even apologize!" to which Nik replied, "But Den, *you* knocked *him* over!"

Levertov and Duncan were both pioneers of "open field" poetry, which, taking cues from both Williams and Pound, was composed "by the phrase," rather than by strict metrical number while remaining finely attentive to musical nuances in the vowels and consonants. Both are well aware that they are figures of a poetry vanguard, but at the same time there is an evident struggle to navigate the polarities of the literary politics of their day and avoid being painted into partisan corners. Working on his book on H.D. (which remains unpublished), Duncan recognizes that his defense of H.D.'s work against dismissive remarks by Randall Jarrell and others galvanizes him and at the same time deflects his attention from the poetry he wishes to explore and celebrate. Shortly after H.D. dies, he writes Levertov in 1963 from San Francisco, where he eventually settles permanently:

When I really go at it, there is no element of the poem that's
not enmeshed in a life that's a dense weave... I'm working
now on the thing about one's Mother. I keep thinking of a
quote I read once from Kerouac – that the world was his
"Mother" – it had been quoted in derision as usual. Yet I
don't know of another as clear statement of the soul's wanting to belong to everything as a child. To be understood! It
means for me being understood by a woman.

And so he was, by Levertov, who, several years younger and less the
poet-scholar, generally defers to his aesthetic distinctions and artic-
ulations. For his part, Duncan loved the physical vitality and specificity of Levertov's work, finding in it a tonic against his own
tendency to eschew the more earthbound realms. Commenting in
the same letter on the recent work of Brother Antoninus, which the
two agreed had jumped offtrack, he writes: "Jess said the book must
have been a religious one because I kept exclaiming – O God! O God
no! O God, not that!"

Those who followed the new American poetry during the late
sixties were dimly aware of a rift between Duncan and Levertov, by
then renowned figures at the height of their powers. *The Letters of
Robert Duncan and Denise Levertov*, scrupulously edited and annotated by Robert J. Bertholf and Albert Gelpi, with a lucid introduction by Gelpi, fulfills the scholar's mandate to set the semipublic
break, which the letters illuminate, in its larger historical context.

Denise Levertov was by nature, it seems, both a poet and an
activist. In 1968, her husband, Mitchell Goodman, along with Dr.
Benjamin Spock and three others, was indicted and convicted of
conspiring against the military draft law (the conviction was over-
turned the following year). Then too, the Goodmans were the parents of a son who was eligible for the draft during these same years.
Understandably, then, Levertov's life and poetry were, for a time,
subsumed by her antiwar activities. The two poets, in turn, close
readers of one another's work as it was written, begin to move apart
because Duncan couldn't countenance what he perceived to be a
strident "us and them" stance in Levertov's antiwar poetry.

Duncan addresses this issue with an eloquence that makes the last third of the book (one as long as *War and Peace* that might have borne the same title) as exhilarating as it is disheartening. Seeing Levertov in an antiwar demonstration in a news segment on television, Duncan was put off by "a force [in her] that, coming on strong, sweeps away all the vital weaknesses of the living identity; the soul is sacrificed to the demotic persona. . ." – and it's not long before this image transmuted for him into Kali Yuga, the death goddess, which, of course, appalled Levertov.

While one can surely find all sorts of Freudian or Jungian subtext in Duncan's reading (not altogether unconscious on his part), he's also probing at the heart of what the creative writer's deepest obligation comprises. As he writes in the same letter of December 1967:

> In South Vietnam, it is not the Liberationists that I identify with but the people of the land who are not fighting to seize political power but are fighting to remain in their daily human lives. It is the villagers in their fight for their village life, the farmer and his ox in their labor that are counterparts of the writer in his labor (to reveal the truth of his vision of things). . .

It's not so much a particular position on the war that Duncan was defending here but rather the sanctity of the life of the creative imagination. While not implicated personally as Levertov was in her husband's and her son's circumstances, Duncan firmly opposed the war. But he believed Levertov, in her social and political commitment to ending the war, had forsaken the mode of consciousness that facilitates the poet's real work. The argument between the two gathers momentum in 1968 – the period of the heaviest death tolls in Vietnam, as well as the murders of Martin Luther King Jr. and Robert Kennedy and the riots at the Democratic National Convention at home. It continues and reaches a crisis point in the early seventies. In a thirteen-page letter, written from October 25th through November 2, 1971, at the Goodmans' retreat in Temple, Maine, Levertov defends her right to speak explicitly in her poetry about the antiwar struggle:

> You (to a degree you must surely be unaware of) set yourself up as an Arbiter of Taste. When do you ever ask, "What do you

think? Do you like. . . ? What do you feel about. . . ?" or say, "It seems to me that. . ."? These forms of address are alien to you because you have so long set yourself up as The Authority, stating your opinions as unquestionable dogmas.

For his part, Duncan sees in any overmastering "position" – whether it's right or wrong – an obstacle to poetry's deepest potential, which, as he understands it, is to provide a crucible in which all the elements may come into play and thereby be illuminated. "The poet's role is not to oppose evil," he writes Levertov, "but to imagine it: what if Shakespeare had opposed Iago, or Dostoyevsky opposed Raskolnikov – the vital thing is that they created Iago and Raskolnikov. And we begin to see betrayal and murder and theft in a new light."

It was, apparently, an unbridgeable chasm, and by the time Duncan, exercising the empathy of his exemplars, begins to edge toward recanting, he has stepped far over the line, in a published interview equating Levertov's antiwar poetry with unconscious sexual sadomasochism.

Duncan died at sixty-nine in 1988 of kidney failure, Levertov at seventy-three in 1997. In their last sporadic letters in the years before Duncan's death, the two are civil but hardly more than that – like two ex-lovers who have hurt one another more than either can quite manage to forgive. (Their love was not "so deep," Levertov writes him in 1979, "that it had not a statute of limitation," and wonders at his failure to apologize for the remarks published years before.) Yet the two decades of their fine romance remain, and one puts down the book moved and chastened by the honor of their shared enterprise in art and in life.

A COMPLICATED MUSE

IN THE EARLY 1960s in New York City, Ted Berrigan, not yet thirty, wrote his masterwork, *The Sonnets*, which leads off this voluminous, definitive collection.* Made up of eighty-eight sonnets, the sequence stands as a sort of literary counterpart to another early postmodern masterwork by another New Yorker undertaken at approximately the same time: Andy Warhol's silk screens of various Campbell soup cans. Both the poet and the painter, that is, fortuitously discovered an unlikely "theater" by which to release and elaborate, to illuminate and play changes upon, sensibilities that would seem to be light-years beyond such old-fashioned, discardable containers.

In Warhol's case, one sees a colorist as pleasing as Matisse in the iconic grid of the soup can: combinations of mauve and purple and green and vermilion never glimpsed on the shelves of the supermarket except perhaps in a dream or, alternatively, seen on early color television sets circa the same period.

In Berrigan's case, the sonnet becomes the vehicle of a sensibility so eclectically learned that the poet in his later years (he died at forty-eight in 1983) would periodically denounce the work as too literary. Recycling lines from poets as various as Henri Michaux and Edwin Arlington Robinson – and prominently including Frank O'Hara, Shakespeare and Rimbaud – he shuffles and reshuffles a pastiche of his New York young adulthood amidst friends, lovers, Pepsis, and pills. Sonnet LV begins with a line of O'Hara's:

---

* *The Collected Poems of Ted Berrigan.* Edited by Alice Notley with Anselm Berrigan and Edmund Berrigan. University of California Press: Berkeley, California. 2005. 749 pp.

Grace to be born and live as variously as possible
White boats   green banks   black dust   atremble
Massive as Anne's thighs upon the page
I rage in a blue shirt at a brown desk in a
Bright room sustained by a bellyful of pills
"The Poems" is not a dream   for all things come to them
Gratuitously   In quick New York we imagine
     the blue Charles
Patsy awakens in heat and ready to squabble
No poems she demands in a blanket command   belly
To hot belly we have laid   serenely white
Only my sweating pores are true in the empty night
Baffling combustions are everywhere!   we hunger
     and taste
And go to the movies   then run home drenched
     in flame
To the grace of the make-believe bed

In different combinations and permutations, many of the lines recur throughout the sequence. One line:

feminine marvelous and tough

is so prototypically Frank O'Hara that I assumed Berrigan had appropriated it until told by the poet that it was entirely his. Able to conjure the chattily cosmopolitan tone of his closest progenitor, he also shared with O'Hara an innately musical ear. But if O'Hara will chart extensive narrative peregrinations ("Joe's Jacket," "A True Account of Talking to the Sun at Fire Island"), Berrigan seldom goes beyond a page or two in his high lyric mode. John Ashbery, to take another of Berrigan's enthusiasms, is mostly about tonal composition – sheets of quasi-ratiocination, as it were – and not really much about the play of vowels and consonants, but Berrigan delighted in him too, as he also delighted in Allen Ginsberg. But perhaps the biggest surprise, comprising a New York School quantum leap, is that Berrigan also embraced the less casual music of the Black Mountain poets (Robert Creeley, Charles Olson, Robert Duncan, etc.). *The*

Sonnets is a milestone, then, in keeping its free-and-easy New York School discursive tone while at the same time advancing a palpable beat that includes incisive musical signatures.

Written several years later, "Tambourine Life," a long poem that appeared in *Mother* magazine in the spring of 1967, comprises a sort of sequel. Berrigan was, as Robert Duncan put it, "a master of pathos," which you see in *The Sonnets* and in the poem about his mother called "Things to Do in Providence." At the same time, he was a comic poet, and "Tambourine Life" holds the full flavor and flux of that side. Divided into seventy sections of open field poetry, the poem is a comedy made up of words and phrases. That is, the words and phrases are the subject of the funniness: what words do, and what they don't do. The whole thing is a kind of high-spirited cartoon of the rational process: each section, most of them very brief, seems to set up a premise and then to demolish it, like a linguistic episode of the Road Runner:

> The apples are red again in Chandler's valley
> redder for what happened there
> never did know what it was
> never did care
>
> *

> Just for the record   I found Mr. Walter Steck
> recently
> at five o'clock in the afternoon
> on Garcia Lorca's birthday
> lying in the gutter
> on his button   *shame*

What might be called the extra-rational spirit of this work seems specific to the literary sixties. Yet for all that, the poet remains on friendly terms with the rational, and not just for the sake of playing on its linguistic limits. There is a sturdy, Johnsonian moral-arbiter side to Berrigan, as when he tells us in "The Great Genius":

> The Great Genius is
> A man who can do the
> Ordinary thing
> When everybody
> Else is going crazy.

Or this, from his poem "I Used to Be But Now I Am":

> I used to be sentimental about myself, & therefore ruthless,
> But now I am, I think, a sympathetic person, although
>   easily amused.

Being human, after all, is to use language to rational ends constantly, and to programmatically divest his work of this dimension might have seemed the sort of exclusion that could have been arrived at only by way of strict rationality. Then too, wanting to be read and enjoyed as a poet, Berrigan may have considered the sort of alternative today represented by the Language Poets to be one that would simply discourage the common reader.

Ted Berrigan was born in Providence, Rhode Island in 1934, the oldest of four children in a working-class Irish Catholic family. His father was chief maintenance engineer at the Ward Baking Company, his mother a bookkeeper and cashier in the public school lunch program. After graduating from the Catholic La Salle Academy, he attended Providence College for a year and then joined the army. He spent sixteen months in Korea before being transferred to Tulsa, now a sergeant. In 1955, he began studying at the University of Tulsa on the GI Bill, and eventually completed a master's thesis there on George Bernard Shaw. In 1959, Berrigan met the future poets Ron Padgett and Dick Gallup, as well as Joe Brainard, the future painter and writer to whom *The Sonnets* is dedicated – all at the time still finishing high school. In 1961, he moved with these friends to New York.

Like Frank O'Hara, whom he already admired and soon knew, Berrigan had a social fluency that could disarm and bring unlikely and disparate parties to his table, and he became the central figure of the second and third generations of poets of the New York School. After the end of his first marriage, having fathered a son and a daughter, he met and married the poet Alice Notley, who, along with their poet sons Anselm and Edmund Berrigan, edited *The Collected Poems*. Almost any of the 749 pages here stands in curious juxtaposition to most of the poetry before us today, a measure of the distance we've kept from the stateside literary sixties.

As both *The Sonnets* and "Tambourine Life" suggest, Berrigan was engaged by all manner and species of "tone" – loving the swift turns he found both in O'Hara and Ashbery, for instance – and almost perpetrated a hoax when his "An Interview with John Cage," published in *Mother*, received an award from the National Endowment for the Arts and was slated to appear in the NEA's newly minted annual, *The American Literary Anthology*. While he took great delight in Cage, the poet was also alert to comedic strains in his persona:

> CAGE: ... I think everybody should be a machine. I think everybody should be like everybody.
> INTERVIEWER: Isn't that like Pop Art?
> CAGE: Yes, that's what Pop Art is, liking things, which incidentally is a pretty boring idea.
> INTERVIEWER: Does the fact that it comes from a machine diminish its value to you?
> CAGE: Certainly not!

The young hipster readership of *Mother* surely got the joke. The piece is daring in its willingness to poke fun at the sacred cows of avant-gardism and Zen Buddhism as well as at the more obvious targets. As the book's publication neared, however, someone in the publisher's office became aware that the interview was made up, comprising quotes from Cage but also from Warhol and William Burroughs, among others. Eventually Cage himself read it, was bemused, but reassured of Berrigan's admiration allowed it to be reprinted with the added disclaimer that it was made up. Berrigan's no less remarkable *Paris Review* interview with Jack Kerouac was in every respect genuine. In effect, whether real or made up, the interview allowed the poet an alternative genre in which to explore his fascination with shifts of tone.

Indeed, so much in these pages seems to be engaged with a kind of high play, both literally and figuratively, and there are moments when one wonders at the inclusion of slighter ephemera. Berrigan was in poor health for more than a decade at the end of his short life – eventually suffering from cirrhosis brought on by complications from drug use, primarily amphetamines – and nothing after *The Sonnets* has the same heft. But the same could be said of Allen Ginsberg's work after *Howl* and *Kaddish*, both written before he was thirty-five. However, in both poets' cases that would miss the generative, well-nigh eucharistic role that seems to be the assigned fate of particular artists.

Berrigan's life combined damaging indulgence with unwavering devotion to poetry, usually at the edge of poverty. After Frank O'Hara's death at forty in 1966, he was the man everyone wanted to see, and he held court judiciously and with a certain solemnity, albeit increasingly from a prone position on a series of day beds in Iowa City, Ann Arbor, Essex, and finally St. Mark's Place on the Lower East Side again. An itinerate poetry professor without tenure, over the years he'd grown enormous.

Near the end of an early poem, "Words for Love," dedicated to his first wife, Sandy Alper, he takes his own measure with remarkable accuracy and prescience:

> At night, awake, high on poems, or pills
> or simple awe that loveliness exists, my lists
> flow differently. Of words bright red
> and black, and blue.   Bosky.   Oubliette.   Dis-
> severed. And O, alas
>
> Time disturbs me. Always minute detail
> fills me up. . .

Knowing the price to be paid for it by the poet and his family, this attention to minute particulars in tone and texture may eventually give one pause. In effect, this poet deconstructed himself – and the more sensible destiny he might have pursued – to follow a complicated muse.

Still, for those of us who came of age in the daunting shadow of Donald M. Allen's watershed anthology *The New American Poetry 1945–1960* (Ginsberg, O'Hara, and company), Berrigan's presence, while ultimately chastening, was a tonic, liberating breath of fresh air. He could respond generously and aptly to so many varieties of poetry – enjoying F. T. Prince one moment and the concrete poems of Ian Hamilton Finlay the next – that he had the rare critical authority of "a mind so fine," as Eliot said of Henry James, "that no idea could violate it."

I first met him in the spring of 1964 at the Greenwich Village party given by Frank O'Hara and Joe LeSueur for the aged Giuseppe Ungaretti. A twenty-year-old native New Yorker, I'd apprenticed myself to the more rigorous Black Mountain poets. Ted, red-bearded and still slim, having recently come across some of my poems, surprised me by responding warmly and breaking the ice.

"But my friends and I – " he added a moment later, smiling, " – we like to tell a few lies in our poems. Or a few jokes, you know? I think you'd be good at that too" – remarks I found both baffling and intriguing.

In addition to the longer works cited, there are a dozen or more lyrics here in which he gives us a music as brightly raucous as a composition by Charles Mingus. Every once in a while, too, comes something as sweet-sorrowful as a passage out of Ellington. Here is the beginning of "Peace":

What to do
               when the day's heavy heart
                              having risen, late
in the already darkening East
               & prepared at any moment, to sink
                                             into the West
surprises suddenly,
               & settles, for a time,
                              at a lovely place

where mellow light spreads
    evenly
      from face to face?

The poem ends:

        And if
she turns your head around
      like any other man,
          go home
and make yourself a sandwich
      of toasted bread, & ham
         with butter
lots of it,
  & have a diet cola,
     & sit down
and write this,
   because you can.

It's good to have this work, lucidly introduced and annotated, at hand in one volume.

CHARLES MINGUS

IN 1979, THE LAST YEAR of his life, Charles Mingus was dismayed when a radio commentator during a rebroadcast of a Mingus concert in New Orleans, praised an early composition of his but got its musical lineage wrong. "I was inspired by Duke Ellington, Debussy, Stravinsky, Bartók," he said. "It had nothing to do with [jazz bassist] Oscar Pettiford."

Ellington was his lifelong idol, and because Mingus also composed for the full orchestral palette, he is Ellington's truest successor. His only rival, Thelonious Monk, was perfectly at home with the small ensemble (although his music is periodically the subject of successful orchestral settings).

I remember seeing Mingus one night at Birdland during the 1960s. He stood with his bass to the left on a bandstand that included reeds, horns, and a rhythm section, and while his players had scores, Mingus would spontaneously call on soloists or indicate whole sections for particular emphasis or unrehearsed interludes. It was as if he was playing his bass and his orchestra simultaneously.

His body of work is among the most emotionally protean with one of the most varied and informed musical pedigrees in American history. In addition to the influences he names above, his compositions embrace gospel, blues, R & B, salsa and Afro-Cuban strains – often in boldly articulated "movements." Works like "Fables of Faubus," "Self Portrait in Three Colors," "Reincarnation of a Love Bird," and "Sue's Changes" are new American classics.

When the New Thing in jazz came along in the sixties, Mingus readily integrated free jazz intervals into the body of his compositions, but we learn in *Tonight at Noon: A Love Story*, his widow Sue Graham Mingus's telling and moving memoir, that he considered

musicians playing exclusively free jazz to be at best incomplete.*
"You don't do anything *all the time,*" he said.

Mrs. Mingus reports a conversation between her husband and
Ellington apropos the New Jazz then at its height, quoting from a
piece Mingus himself wrote: "'Duke, why don't you, me, and Dizzy
[Gillespie] and Clark Terry and Thad Jones get together and make
an avant garde record?' Duke's reply was very quick: 'Why should
we go back that far? Let's not take music back that far, Mingus. Why
not just make a modern record?'"

Mingus died at fifty-six of amyotrophic lateral sclerosis, com-
monly known as Lou Gehrig's disease. Even so, his body of work is the
second largest in jazz, only exceeded by Ellington's, and includes
major compositions still to be recorded.

Like his music, Charles Mingus's life was multifaceted and inclusive,
running the gamut from a childhood and adolescence in the Watts
ghetto of Los Angeles to concerts in the capitals of Europe and the
Americas. There were friendships with, among others, Norman
Mailer and Joni Mitchell, who, late in Mingus's life, became a collaborator. Sue Mingus records her husband's first meeting with
Mitchell, which occurred when he was already fatally ill:

> They were an unlikely couple, Joni and Charles: Joni, a singer
> who didn't read music, who refused to risk her gifts or her
> intuition by submitting them to formal study. And Charles,
> who, as a teenager in Los Angeles, studied composition and
> music theory with the legendary Lloyd Reese, and mastered
> the classical bass with Herman Rheinshagen, the retired
> principal bassist of the New York Philharmonic. Joni's musi-
> cal talents fell into place on their own, a natural outgrowth of
> her poetry.
>
>   "You're the hillbilly singer," Charles . . . said to her straight-
> faced from his wheelchair when she first walked into our liv-
> ing room. She stopped dead at the entrance and stared at him

---

* Sue Graham Mingus, *Tonight at Noon: A Love Story*. Pantheon: New York.
2002. 272 pp.

without speaking. He'd caught her off guard. She was standing beside Don Alias, tall, black, and handsome, the jazz per-
cussionist who was living with her then. She was taller than I
had imagined and looked surprisingly serious. Suddenly she
relaxed. She looked at Charles slyly and burst out laughing.
They liked each other from the start.

In the fall of 1964, at the Manhattan funeral of my friend Steve
Reichman, who had died in Europe over his summer break from
New York University, I was surprised when it was announced that
Charles Mingus, unseen behind the proscenium curtain, would play
a solo bass eulogy. The austerely beautiful solo, and Mingus's gen-
erosity to the family of his young fan, was a moving gesture at the
abrupt end of a promising life. Earlier that same year Sue Graham had
been introduced to Mingus at the Five Spot, the Greenwich Village
jazz club where he was appearing. She was married to an Italian
artist at the time and was the mother of a young son and daughter.

A Milwaukee debutante and Smith graduate, Graham had broken with her fifties upbringing and embarked on her own adventur-
ous life odyssey during a visit to Europe. And now she was living in
Manhattan as the sixties began to go into gear. Pursued by the
tumultuous, imperious but also loving jazz legend, she was alternately overwhelmed and repelled. For years the two, married first
by Allen Ginsberg in an impromptu ceremony at an Upper East Side
townhouse and a second time at City Hall, maintained separate
addresses. But Sue Mingus eventually not only merged her life with
her husband's, but in the two decades since his death has become
the central figure in the perpetuation and proliferation of his musical legacy, releasing his performances on her own label – started to
thwart rampant bootlegging of his music – as well as initiating the
first large ensemble to perform his music posthumously.

One of this book's many pleasures is the record, rendered in intimate close-up, of the loving camaraderie in the African-American
musical community:

[Mingus] remembered a concert in Europe long ago when
Dizzy was playing on the bandstand and he was standing below,

some distance away, thinking about Dizzy's importance and hoping Dizzy would live forever. Although his back was turned, Dizzy swung around suddenly and asked out loud where all the love he felt was coming from. Then he looked straight at Charles.

"You really do love me, don't you?" Dizzy said. "I felt just then like I was in heaven!"

When Mingus arrives one night at the Village Vanguard to hear Miles Davis, the trumpeter "came over, wiped Charles's face with his hands (wiping his own blackness onto Charles's mongrel skin, as Charles later explained), and tussled his hair. Then Miles headed for the bandstand.

"Charles smiled happily, 'I don't feel lonesome anymore,' he said."

At the same time, Mingus practiced what he called "creative anger" and would often berate members of his audience for making disruptive noise during his performances. When his friend Timothy Leary wanted him to try LSD, which he believed would allow "people [to] shed their old neurotic imprints and begin again," his wife reports that "Mingus was less interested in shedding his imprint than in changing the world's."

"I know I'm not perfect," he told Leary, "but I don't want to play bass any different. I don't want to write music any different."

When disease strikes, he suffers its swift, merciless advance with bravery and humor, while at the same time driving his wife to her limits and beyond. Beginning with Western medicine, they soon look to alternative varieties, including a stop at a clinic in Montreux where Mingus receives "a dozen injections from the organs of an unborn lamb. Lamb liver cells. Lamb heart cells. Lamb kidney cells. Lamb pancreas." Sharing a hospital room with separate beds, Mrs. Mingus awakens early the next morning:

In the semi-darkness I watched him as he lay in bed. He looked crucified. He could barely move his body. . . I realized his eyes were open and that he had been watching me as well.

Suddenly his mouth quivered and emitted a long, low sound: "B-a-a-a-a-a-a-a-a-a-a-a-a. . ." he said.

With a small team in tow, acting on a tip from Gerry Mulligan, the couple's last stop is Mexico, where they eventually take up residence at a rented villa in Cuernavaca, and Mingus is treated by a seventy-two-year-old female Indian witch doctor named Pachita and her lieutenants. Her treatment culminates with a miraculously (or fraudulently) bloodless surgery. Virtually paralyzed but still meeting each day with appetite, Mingus dies not long afterward of a heart attack. Honoring his wishes, his widow makes a pilgrimage to scatter his ashes over the Ganges, "certain that the raw air beneath the dark range of the Himalayas was made for the life of the spirit and for reincarnation, as he believed."

To listen to the music of Charles Mingus is to hear darkness and light, pain and jubilation, beauty and beast, in an enchanted musical continuum. Sue Mingus survives and perpetuates her husband's legacy with a loving, exacting portrait: *Tonight at Noon*, titled after one of her husband's compositions, has the emotional fluency and power of Mingus's own music.

ANDY WARHOL:
I'LL BE YOUR MIRROR

1

DURING THE 1960S, Andy Warhol was interviewed on television by the art critic Alan Solomon. Warhol was seated on a bar stool and dressed in dark jeans and a black leather jacket, and as always had a gentle demeanor and spoke softly. Solomon was asking questions from a chair in front of the artist, Warhol seated above him as if on a makeshift pedestal. The questions were the art-savvy currency of the critic, but Warhol answered monosyllabically, mostly with umm's or yes's. Then after a third or fourth exchange, he broke this pattern.

"Would you," he said softly to Solomon, "give me the answers to the questions, too?"

A passage in John Giorno's memoir, *You've Got to Burn to Shine*, tells of the poet's visit to Warhol's earliest New York studio in the East 80s, where he encounters for the first time a giant "star" portrait (of Elvis).

How exhilarating that breakthrough must have been to the young, transplanted native of Pittsburgh. A year or so earlier, Warhol had been hand drawing advertisements for women's shoes. He drew the best shoes of anyone in the business, the legend runs. A graduate of his native city's Carnegie Mellon University, he'd moved to New York with his classmate the painter Philip Pearlstein and was making ends meet. As he evolved as an artist, he put aside painting and drawing to make silk screens of public domain photographs, effectively abandoning a personal hand in his work, except that his sense of color remained brilliantly in play. He also continued to make color accents by hand throughout his œuvre.

Most crucially, what he took from his commercial into his fine art was commercialism itself – ramping it up to portray an electric civilization in which fame is both subject and product. A deceptively quiet-spoken imperialist, anything was fair game for his œuvre: Marilyn Monroe and the electric chair; car wrecks and Elizabeth Taylor; the ten most wanted men (by the FBI, surely a Warhol joke); a life-size wood replica of a Brillo box (in fact hundreds of them); a Campbell soup can utilized as a grid for a color-field workout also seen in his multipaneled self-portrait. Using iconic images, he made more multiples of them, enacting on a smaller scale the process that had produced their fame in the first place. Today, images he made are on refrigerator magnets.

2

A guest at Warhol's first "factory" on East 47th Street would be invited to sit down for a "screen test" in front of a movie camera on a tripod. The artist would set the lights and then let a three-minute reel of film run from beginning to end. There were no lines to read and nothing otherwise to do, as if the subject were asked to sit for a still portrait and instead was filmed.

While a single image can suggest the visceral inner nature, these portraits comprise neurological *narratives*. How many times a subject blinks or swallows or moves his or her head renders the portrait extraordinarily intimate, as if a Rembrandt were to start breathing.

If Warhol presents electronic time in multiplying a single image in his works on canvas, in the "screen tests" we see and feel linear time nakedly – like Beckett without words.

In *Sleep*, John Giorno, Warhol's boyfriend at the time, sleeps for six hours while the camera records it from a single angle. In *Empire State*, another silent epic again from a single camera angle, we see the tallest building in Manhattan go through the night and into the dawn. It's curiously comforting to know these films were made, and more or less unnecessary to watch them, as if we now have mortality packaged, in the can, if we should ever need to confirm it.

* * *

Next came "talkies."

My Hustler features Paul America and Ed Hood, a Cambridge professor. There's the buff America at the bathroom mirror and the rumpled balding professor nearby – and the beach just outside. It's dazzlingly off-kilter and dead-on. Our America.

In the split-screen magnum opus *Chelsea Girls*, there are things going on in various rooms of the Chelsea Hotel. The sound track comes from one or the other of the two separate rooms that divide the screen. Mostly inchoate or incomprehensible dramas unfold while the camera finds subjects of its own to contemplate: a bureau and the back of someone's head in the frame . . . zooming in on a corner of the room with nothing in it.

Here is the disinterested mind of the artist apprehending a culture in a seismic shift. An equal opportunity observer, if someone wanted to make a scene, Warhol would oblige by filming it, i.e., Ondine's explosive rant in *Chelsea Girls* when a young woman offends him – a dramatic high-point in a goofily routine chronicle, perhaps Warhol's own testimony to his famous statement: "In the future, everyone will be famous for 15 minutes" – a prediction likely to prove out only in the event that the mechanics of fame were in the hands of Warhol himself.

Beauty Number 2, starring Edie Sedgwick, and *Nude Restaurant*, starring Viva and Taylor Mead, are, literally, situation comedies. In *Beauty Number 2*, Edie lies on a bed with a young-man/boy-toy while Chuck Wein, Edie's Cambridge friend and Svengali, is off-camera making increasingly provoking comments to her. On her way to getting upset, Edie and her partner on the bed assume fetching poses in dishabille.

Nude Restaurant is a place where nude patrons are served by nude waitresses. The situation is given in the first frame and, dramatically speaking, after an initial jolt, seems stillborn. But this is to underestimate those two inveterate troupers of underground cinema: Taylor Mead, the fey Chaplinesque figure of dozens of films never shown above 14th Street; and Viva, the elegant and witty young lapsed Catholic, a sort of psychedelic Mary McCarthy.

The final sequence – a large portion of the film – was another single-angle shot trained on Viva's talking head, while in a lower corner of the screen Mead alternately listens and zones out. She is speaking exhaustively about the clitoral versus the vaginal orgasm: whether there is a real distinction, the pros and cons of either versus the other. Mead, neither riveted nor quite willing to detach, takes in particular turns in the argument and is otherwise occupied with his own thoughts, but always with companionable good humor, a half-smiling elf.

If there's a single scene in American film that can stand with anything in world cinema since the Nouvelle Vague, this one gets my vote. A talking head, even a brilliant one, can get old after a few minutes. A talking head with a silent but intermittently responsive companion also head-on in the frame is something else. It affected one with the same kind of exhilaration one knew in, say, hearing Jimi Hendrix for the first time.*

On June 3, 1968, Warhol was shot and critically wounded in the offices of his new studio on Union Square by a marginal figure among the factory crowd, Valerie Solanis. A militant, lesbian feminist who had a script she wanted Warhol to film, Solanis was the author of *The S.C.U.M.* [Society for Cutting Up Men] *Manifesto*, an often incisive rant against the patriarchy, which, she wrote, reduced a woman to nothing more than "a hot water bottle with tits."

While Solanis didn't succeed in killing Warhol, her attempt on his life put an end to his career as a filmmaker. Henceforth, all Warhol's films would be directed by Paul Morrissey, a gifted but more conventional filmmaker who succeeded in commercializing the line – *Trash, Flesh, Heat*, etc. – at the expense of most of what made the artist's own films both ineffable and unforgettable.

In a few years, Warhol had created his own studio system and concomitant "super-stars": Ultraviolet, Ondine, Ingrid Superstar, Jane Forth, Gerard Malanga, Mary Woronov, Taylor Mead, Paul America, Edie Sedgwick, Eric Emerson, Candy Darling, Viva, Joe Dallesandro, Brigid Polk, International Velvet, Holly Woodlawn, et al. – and they

---

* Years after its premiere, when *Nude Restaurant* was shown at Film Forum in New York, the long scene at the end had been truncated and had nothing like its original power. Are there multiple prints of this film in the Warhol archives?

comprised his repertory company. The template being the Hollywood studio system, the artist presided over it like a taciturn, very
permissive Louis B. Mayer. Instead of entreating his stars to stay
out of trouble (Judy Garland said Mayer could cry "ball-bearing
tears" at will), Warhol would hasten the mischief on.

3

In his multipaneled self-portrait, we see Warhol's face as if in the
serial exposures of a strobe light show – red, green, blue, etc., the
features at times almost lost, the face becoming a medium of light.
The artist, as the Solomon interview attests, was unable or unwill-
ing to talk in art-critic parlance about the significance of his work
and rather became its living annex. Then too, he famously allowed
the actor Allen Midgette to impersonate him for a scheduled college appearance: he made a living multiple of himself.

The attempt on his life, and the subsequent days when his life
hung in the balance, was a strange reversal of fortune. Now Warhol,
who had created a wizardly miniature of our media, became the real-
time focus of the New York daily tabloids – as if his œuvre turned
inside out.

From Claes Oldenburg to Roy Lichtenstein, from Tom Wesselmann
to James Rosenquist, Pop Art, the new movement in painting, was
an efflorescence of sensibility and technical accomplishment that
quickly claimed a large public. At the same time, among the major
figures, Warhol stood apart. While there was a pervasive sense that
the movement put paid to Abstract Expressionism's romantic image
of the artist as a tortured outrider of his time – Jackson Pollock being
Exhibit One – Warhol went the farthest in the other direction, in the
process claiming attention that exceeded everyone else's. A leading
Pop artist, he became a pop *figure*, appearing with members of his
entourage on *The Tonight Show*.

Paradoxically, he accomplished this by making a public specta-
cle of having not only no obvious personal demons to wrestle, but
being perhaps the mildest, least assertive personality ever to assume
a central position in public consciousness. While his work had pres-

ence that rivaled anything in the museums, his own presence was a study in low-wattage affability both benign and inscrutable. Who was he, exactly? He showed up, becoming a familiar face at New York parties and openings, and reliably lent a hand on holidays at his church soup kitchen. At the end of the night, he went back to a home kept for him by his mother, Julia Warhola, a Polish immigrant whose beautiful handwriting he'd imported for the copy in his shoe ads.

While his Pop Art colleagues were demonstrably masters of their craft, Warhol made the *mechanics* of reproduction central to his œuvre. No one else did this, or surely not to the degree that Warhol did, and his industrialized, depersonalized means might have eclipsed his ends, except for the power and beauty of what he made. That is to say, whatever his medium or its means, he remained pre-eminently an artist – the lone visual artist of his day to rival in impact the leading figures of the music scene: The Beatles, Bob Dylan, and the Rolling Stones. In their different ways, all laid down a template of consciousness and sensibility that would impress an international public as forcefully as Picasso and Gershwin, Sinatra and Jackson Pollock had earlier.

In the Kleinian, post-Freudian school of psychoanalysis, the good-enough mother (a designation of the British analyst Donald Winnicott), is one who takes in the infant's projected terror, and, in meeting it with both empathy and equanimity, detoxifies it. The great artist may be doing something similar: giving back to us an image of ourselves that while it acknowledges our full range of colors, dark as well as light, allows beauty into the equation.

"He had a mind so fine," T. S. Eliot famously wrote of Henry James, "that no idea could violate it." – a line that might also apply to Warhol. Not that either James or Warhol would disdain ideas per se, but that they would apprehend them perceptually – James tracking his character's thoughts with the same equanimity as he would describe a landscape; and Warhol benignly asking Alan Solomon for the exact intellectual responses the critic wanted to hear, in effect being available to make a copy of Solomon's mind.

OCCUPATION: WRITER

OCCUPATION: WRITER *

I GREW UP the son of a famous writer, grew up in his shadow in a general sense, except for two fortuitous graces. They say the universe never gives you more than you can handle, and I believe it (sometimes). Those two saving graces are, first, that astrologically speaking, I had many planets in Leo and so was absurdly full of confidence when I wasn't struck numb with my own incapacities. And the other, and perhaps the decisive factor, was that I had the honor of being a member of the generation that came of age in the sixties. I wish that every generation could be so honored. I certainly wish it for my own children, of the so-called Generation X, because it was for me and for a great many of us, I think, so empowering – such a great boost of confidence seemed to come forward to us out of that complex of circumstances we call the 1960s. We felt special – that we mattered, that we might have an impact on the way things were – and I believe all young people deserve to feel that way and know that more often than not they don't.

In my case, it meant, for instance, that I no longer had to wallow in the shadows of being the son of a famous man. I was rather, in the argot of those days, "what was happening, baby." The initiating incident. Act One, you might say. I exulted in feeling empowered, took multiple steps in several different directions ... and along this charmed way made a mistake.

A mistake for a writer – for a writer like I was, anyway – is a serious situation. Let's not forget all those planets in Leo. Suddenly it came to me that my first two books of poetry, which had been pub-

---

* Delivered on April 26, 2000, at Boston University as the Fourteenth Abraham S. Burack Lecture of the Friends of Libraries at Boston University.

lished in fairly quick succession by Random House, contained a fundamental error. What pain! I went to sleep with it, woke up without it, and then it hit me again, although everything in me wanted to forego it – wanted it to be a momentary misapprehension. Now, I say this from the advanced perspective of several intervening decades: It *was* a misapprehension. There are no real errors in this dimension – there is only growth. But you can't have growth without the perception of error, or anyway without the perception that a change is desirable.

That first time was hard, and I owe a great deal to my wife, Gailyn, who allowed me to be wrong, who seemed at times to insist that I couldn't *not* be wrong, and thus permitted me to experience the reality that being wrong and being dead were not the same thing. One went on breathing, one continued to have energy. One needed only to go on and do more.

And that brings me to another grace, for a Libra, which is my sun sign, perhaps the preeminent grace: a partner, Gailyn. She was and is, simply, an equal who understood things in a way similar to the way I understood them and then understood other things that I had no inkling of and communicated that I would do well to try to pick up on them. A great lifelong companion is perhaps *the* gift life can bestow. For me, I can say unequivocally that Gailyn made my life as a writer and, even more importantly, my life as a man. Librans are creatures of relationships, as I say, and for me that was the primary means of the process of tempering, of civilizing, that deepened my life with each passing day, week, month, and year.

What are those of us who write trying to do? The Scots poet Ian Hamilton Finlay tells us, "The best a writer writes is beautiful / Forget the mad and dutiful." Still we have it on Keats's good authority that what is true and what is beautiful may be one and the same. The question is how is one supposed to write that, the true and/or the beautiful? How does one get to it?

A little while after the sixties, it came to me that the way one might be able to do that – or to try to do it – was to trust oneself, to trust one's judgments, one's instincts, one's *voice*, should it make evidence of itself. "You don't have to be right," Allen Ginsberg said. "You just have to be candid."

One of the things I'd learned by now was that for me, always trying to get the scales to balance, the so-called psychoactive drugs popular in my generation were not a good idea. My father once wrote me: "Just be yourself – that will do it." It's funny. I once saw my father, in London in 1966, after he'd spent the night gambling and drinking. He'd misplaced his key and at dawn knocked on the door of the apartment where he and my sister Lucy and I were all staying together for a month or two, and I got up off the living room sofa, where I slept, and answered the door; and he smiled apologetically and mumbled something about the misplaced key; and he was, it seemed to me, so saturated in alcohol that he literally exuded an essence of booze from all his pores – but he wasn't drunk. I think I can say I never saw him drunk, and in that sense, at least, he was always himself. Pop was a Virgo, an earth sign, with a Taurus rising, another earth sign. He could handle the booze and in fact was never terribly interested in it.

But I'm virtually all air and fire signs – and of course air will feed a fire – so I didn't have that ability to remain grounded in the same way. I needed to domesticate myself, so to put it, and that meant no psychedelic lift-offs. I was already airborne. It would have been redundant. I love what the late Michael Bennett, who choreographed *A Chorus Line*, once said about his hometown, Buffalo, New York. "Committing suicide in Buffalo," he said, "was redundant." It was like one of those great junior high vocabulary examples.

This issue of being oneself and trusting oneself is very close to the issue of knowing oneself – for a writer perhaps the fundamental issue, certainly for a writer such as I was, one of the near-extinct genus without affiliation in either academia or the media. Louis Zukofsky wrote in his long poem *A*, "The best man learns of himself / To bring rest to others." As my own boss, the matter was very close at hand. Then too, my generation had not enamored itself in the corridors of power. We had reversed the circuitry of the American postwar economic and psychological boom – those years of the unself-conscious American empire. Instead we had taken to heart tenets of the Declaration of Independence, the Constitution, and the

Bill of Rights and put ourselves in harm's way in a nation conceived in the rhetoric of liberty that yet reserved fundamental, inalienable rights to the hierarchy. "All the children / were taught the pledge of Allegiance," the late poet Edward Dorn wrote, "and the land was pledged / to private use, the walnut dropped in the autumn on the ground / green, and lay black in the dead grass in the spring."

If one doesn't write for *Time*, or for NBC, one has the op-ed page, the book review, the poem, the story, the essay, the novel. In effect, one is trying to learn how to behave in a job for which there is no particular description or career track. There isn't a union; there are no benefits, no retirement, nothing but the dream one has somehow been given as an inheritance of one's time, perhaps having misunderstood it – the dream of being a writer.

When we speak of the American writer – the unaffiliated writer – perhaps we are speaking of one hundred individuals, those who earn their livings in that profession. There are thousands of geologists, plumbers, photographers, doctors, taxi-cab drivers, pornographers, stock brokers, petty thieves, drug dealers, and newspaper and television writers, in no particular order. There are perhaps as many independent self-supporting American writers as there are trapeze artists.

I had the great advantage and the erstwhile discomfort of having a father who had not only taken this journey before me but also had established himself, against great odds, as one of the hundred or so. At about this time, as the seventies took hold, things began to change in me with respect to my father and to predecessors in general. I began to take deeper sustenance from their various examples. I was now by hook or by crook, or any other means, writing. Having started with poetry, I went on to write op-ed pieces and reviews, and then novels, biographies, nonfiction novels, and memoirs. And for a while, my father, who died in 1981 at the age of seventy-two, was also simultaneously writing, and occasionally he would say something, send me a bulletin across the years as it were, that would give me pause and help me understand things in a larger way.

In the 1970s, when he published a memoir and went on *The Today Show*, among several other television shows, his sales multiplied geometrically. He sold four or five times the number of books he had been used to selling at that point in his career. "We live in a bullshit culture," he remarked about that boost in sales at the time, not angry about it, only bemused. He was an early entry, so to speak, in what would later be known as the Oprah Club. But let's not forget that as an American writer of the Depression years, William Saroyan had known the kind of mythic literary fame without television that only Kerouac knew after its advent.

Around this time, too, Joyce's survival prescription for the writer, "silence, exile, and cunning," began to resonate in me. It grew on me that I was not necessarily a welcome guest in the higher offices of my society. I was, by definition it seemed, an outlander, and, in literary circles, too, as a writer to whom controversy was not a stranger, as likely as not to be considered one. Gore Vidal has pointed out that writing is the only profession in which one is reviewed by one's competitors, and this can lead to unfortunate career collisions. The first large review I received in *The New York Times Book Review* was a slam by a writer a little older than I whom I've never had another occasion to read. The second big review was a rave, but it was followed closely by a slam in the daily *Times* by a writer I admired, though obviously he had his blind spots. Now both of the books I refer to were major acts of my life, major works, and in the bad reviews, I was dealt with only a little less severely than I might have expected to be, had I, for instance, committed a robbery.

And I hasten to add, I was one of the lucky ones. My books were reviewed big, three times, and one of the reviews was a rave. I've seen young writers summarily slaughtered in the "In Brief" section of the *Times Book Review*, and these are writers, good writers too, from whom we may never hear again as a result of such reviews. So I'll come right out now and say it.

America is not particularly fond of writers. I don't mean Americans, my fellow citizens. I believe many of them truly and touchingly love writers and reading and books. I'm talking about official America: those corridors of power again. Writers are not genuinely welcome there. After all, as Doris Lessing pointed out, the writer may be the last single voice to enter the public discourse without being qualified, edited, or rewritten entirely by affiliations and officialdoms of one sort or another. She or he stands apart.

Let's quickly add that that isn't necessarily a heroic posture – or rather, heroic though it might on occasion be, it can also be dangerous to the writer, a liability that can make learning and growing even more difficult than it already is. Here's a personal example. In the 1980s, I began to get around as a writer, earning more and being better published and writing as well as I had ever written, but a curious thing had started to happen to me. Having by now written quite a bit and published much of it, I began to feel a little depleted, a little spent, as though I had used up the better part of my writer's capital, to use Henry James's phrase. And I was uncertain about how to go about renewing my resources or finding new ones. I looked with secret envy on the commuters who crowded the L.A. freeways at rush hour each morning, all of them securely stitched into the American mainstream, or so it seemed to me. I wondered what things were like in their offices. I was in my mid-forties now, married and the father of three children, and yet I had no world, as it were, aside from whatever project I could come up with in the hope that it would interest a publisher.

Indeed, isolation can be very much a liability – and can be enforced by success as much or more than by failure. Failure makes a man get up in the morning and head out the door to find answers; it reinforces one's connection with one's fellows, with the larger world.

As it happens, no sooner had I begun entertaining such fugitive thoughts about what was going on in the mythic offices of America than my career went into involuntary, massive collapse. I say involuntary, and that was certainly how it felt at the time, but now I have to wonder if I wasn't perversely – or perhaps not perversely, but perseveringly – an active collaborator in the process. Sometimes a writer may need to do something that seems damnably inconvenient and even outright crazy to continue to be a writer. In my situation, I believe it was largely an involuntary, or let's say an unconscious, process but that it was dictated by a deeper necessity I recognized at a gut level. I burned bridges, with a certain profligacy, for no clear reason.

To make a long story short, then, in my mid-forties I began a new phase in which I took the sort of jobs that usually *precede* literary careers, later to be recounted in those book jacket biographical notes. Airport van driver . . . editor of medical reports on job-related stress for workers' compensation claims . . . public relations receptionist . . . public relations account executive . . . and finally, Public Information Officer for a federally funded job training program in Ventura County. I wouldn't have taken any of these jobs unless I had to, and at the same time I had a gut instinct that each one was an opportunity to renew my resources as a writer – that they comprised individually and en masse my own *next step*.

This is an ineffable of my experience, and it may be outside any parameters of literary vocation that we recognize, but I've found that in the unfolding phases of my adult life, there is often something I will perceive either clearly or dimly that I must do next. This is something that looms before me as – to make a convenient image of it – a door, for example, upon which I must knock to enter the next phase of my life. Once it was literally a door, a neighbor's door, one I approached with some trepidation, and with good reason, for I needed to knock at it and precipitate a crisis less for the neighbor – this crisis, that is – than for me. It was very uncomfortable – the event and its aftermath – and I believe necessary, with a long-term positive outcome.

Can I say that I knew that by doing this uncomfortable thing I would become a better writer? I don't think I knew that at the time. But in my response to the crisis, over the long aftermath, I recognized certain alternative responses that would or would not represent a deeper commitment to being a writer, and I opted to follow those alternatives that would deepen the commitment. The vocation of writer, after all, like any vocation – surgeon, gambler, singer-songwriter – is identifiably, especially as one gets deeper into it, a nervous system. That is to say, a certain kind of nervous system will foster and enforce one's best abilities in the arena one chooses. A surgeon, for instance, is going to be careful not to drink too much the evening before an operation. The chemistry of the writer may be fostered similarly. Norman Mailer recently remarked that he believed the ideal psychological state for a working writer was a low-grade depression, and I understood what he meant. For one tends to be a little more sensitive, in my experience, a little more open, when one is slightly depressed. I also like something Kurt Vonnegut said in a commencement address: Do something every day that scares you a little.

As for results, after six or seven years in the American work-force, getting to know all about the way things were at the office and on the freeway, it seemed I'd learned what I'd needed to learn to arrive at the next threshold in my work.

Here is the situation I encountered in my last station in that series of jobs. I had a partitioned cubicle in an office with sixty or seventy other workers, and in the cubicle was a desk, a computer that wasn't attached to a network and therefore could not be monitored, and a telephone. This large office was occupied by employees of another agency, my own immediate supervisors being at another location. My job involved coordinating and making presentations about gov-ernment services available to laid-off workers and also included writing press releases and various kinds of reports, and there were interims during which none of that, or anything else, needed imme-diate attention. One afternoon in the cubicle during one of those interims, I started to write a play. The play virtually exploded in my computer monitor, I should say.

There is, I think, a resident genius in form itself, in the right form when it manifests at the right time in the right place. It might be a poem the words of which seem to be virtually stitched into one's breathing; it might be an essay in which things finally achieve elu-sive equilibrium. Or it might be a play, in which voices and histories, a kind of personal music of life, come across in a way they never have before.

There I was, in my cubicle, with coworkers going by. With cer-tain of the coworkers, too, I was coordinating presentations, so there was always that little buzz of danger in the fact that my computer monitor was full of characters and dialogue that had nothing to do with the Employment Development Department or the Job Train-ing Partnership Act, of which I was the vested representative to the citizens of Ventura County.

But it was no more than a buzz because my coworkers would no more look into my monitor than into my desk drawer, and if I believed for a moment that they might, I could close up the file. To summa-rize, then: I believed I'd pretty much run dry creatively, and I had a deep if virtually preconscious notion that I needed to step into the workforce and find out about the real American world of those daily commuters on the freeway. I did that, joined that world, and after six or seven years – and as I say I wouldn't have done *any* of this if I hadn't had an urgent need of money because of burning those various bridges, projects going down in flames, et al. – after six or seven years, I was being paid by the government as I sat writing first one play and then half of a second one in a series that would eventually comprise five plays, and writing with the tremendous excitement that happens a few times in the course of one's working life: the sensation that one has struck gold. If I had tried to imagine beforehand such a salutary and beneficent scenario, I don't think I could have come close.

So I believe in a process that might be called God, or the universe ("the universe is the messiah," Michael McClure says in his poem "99 Theses"), or the Higher Power. Edmund Wilson refers somewhere to "the moral model of the death and resurrection," seeing in the Christian paradigm, it occurs to me, the process by which, for instance, we come to learn any new thing: "dying" at the level of ego in order to take in new information and then "being reborn" with the new knowledge. What is the cause of death? The Buddhist says the cause of death is birth. Likewise, in the Christian paradigm, death leads to resurrection, rebirth. And so it seemed to happen to me as a writer in that EDD office in Oxnard. Those were exciting days.

These last several years, teaching in the Graduate Writing Program at USC in Los Angeles, as well as conducting private workshops and giving talks and seminars, I've looked more closely than before at my own literary tradition and process, which I've tried to characterize in certain ways here and to which I'll now add the issue of knowledge of the larger world, the historical reality of one's time, if you will, as it evolved over the years of my engagement with writing.

Was it E. M. Forster who said that as a writer progresses, it's natural to try to embrace more and more of this larger world in his or her writing? As I've tried to characterize, I began with questions of self, of personal identity, the feeling of being overshadowed by a famous father, and then had an experience of a sort of historical intervention, the sixties, which delivered me out of those shadows and set me on the stage of the larger historical moment. In that

sense, I was aware early on that history could be a potent and sometimes decisive factor in one's evolution. Publishing per se was never
easier for me than it was in the sixties – well, it was easier for most
writers in those days. But the honeymoon was over quickly, and I
stood as bemused as my father had been when he saw the effect of
his TV appearances on his book sales. What, or where, exactly, was
the culture in all this?

That same question resonates even more crucially today. We've
seen a closing of ranks against the individual voice the writer represents, a kind of corporate vise grip on the channels of communication that even as they multiply seem only to provide more of the
same. However, as we saw last December at the World Trade Organization protests in Seattle, e-mail can be a potent resource for
protesting that world which an unfettered free market, without an
ethical or cultural base line of any kind, will foster. This is a world
in which the transnational corporation will biogenetically alter a
seed for a particular kind of food, so that the corporation will be
able to hold the patent on that food. The late Jean-Michel Basquiat,
the celebrated American painter of the 1980s, has the word *milk* in
one of his paintings, and in the upper right corner of the word has
also painted the little copyright symbol. Exactly right. Quietly, with
poker faces, they are taking out a patent on broccoli. Could Woody
Allen do something with this? It's good for profits – regardless of
what biogenetic messing around may do to the food itself, the soil,
the environment . . . or us, the people who are obliged to eat this new
idea. Let me add that *The New York Times*, with which I have my own
issues, has covered this story with great circumspection, if at all.

Marshall McLuhan told us back in the sixties, "There is no in-
evitability so long as there is a willingness to consider alternatives."
We are now smack in that brave new world we've been warned off
by our writers for a century or more. This is a world in which 350 bil-
lionaires have as much wealth as half the world's population. Publishing is only a single chess piece in the big international game of
high finance. Rupert Murdoch's News Corporation routinely can-
celed a book critical of China's human rights record scheduled by
HarperCollins, Murdoch's American publishing arm, because the
chief was interested in China's media markets. What is true and/or

important may itself be subject to redefinition, now, at the whim of the CEO.

Not a good time for the independent writer. By now, though, that's an old story. And in the meantime we've learned a bit more about the way the world works that fosters, rather than hampers, the best that we know in ourselves. The same world in which the CEO of Disney, Michael Eisner, had a salary in 1998 of $278,000 an hour (a student of mine remarked that he could work until lunch and then retire) also includes the many unsung heroes of our day. I'd love to see a new magazine called *Other People* about the people we never meet in our media who do important work with energy and spirit and conscience, some of whom became my friends and exemplars when I took that series of jobs.

I'll end with a brief story I wrote in the period when I was largely engaged in work other than writing, a story that remembers, I realize now, an earlier exemplar of that work-a-day world. Here is a figure, then, of that ever mysterious, generative world out there, which has gone on and continues to go on despite any and all interference. It's said that the survival of the planet depends on such figures and that few if any of them are well-known.

THE GENIUS*

It was on an evening in the early seventies, still light out, that I boarded the bus for Bolinas at Seventh and Market Streets in San Francisco. The driver was an African-American, tall and straight-backed in his seat, chewing gum, with a jaunty improvisatory quality about him. You sensed he was in a certain groove. The usual driver seemed to take the job as a routine diminution, a strictly mechanical operation, but this man was putting his personal, rhythmical stamp on it.

I was a new father, and my whole idea was to become a dependable citizen. The sixties had been a kind of deconstruction for my generation – we had melted away our personalities, getting down to

---

* From *Artists In Trouble: New Stories*. Black Sparrow Press: Santa Rosa, CA. 2001.

nothing at all – but now I wanted to feel something solid in myself. It wasn't an easy thing for me to feel, and paradoxically just then, with the sixties over, it probably got harder.

I took a window seat and looked out at the twilit streets with their after-work rush of pedestrians as we moved toward Lombard Street and the Golden Gate Bridge. The ride to Bolinas is fairly routine until you start up Mount Tamalpais in Mill Valley. From there it's a long climb with turn after turn and then a long descent, with as many more turns, into Stinson Beach.

All of us, his passengers, knew immediately that we were in the hands of a special driver. We moved both faster and more decisively than normally. Then as we started the climb up Mount Tam and at the same time darkness began to settle in, it was as if we were inside something infinitely greater than a commuter bus on an evening run. The ride was like an enactment of an extraordinary, overseeing, protective power: it was like being a passenger inside cosmic grace.

In the darkness at the front, he sat erect but loose-limbed, turning the steering wheel – which lay just above his knees in a slightly pitched horizontal position – left and then right, right and then left again, as he negotiated turn after turn.

For a while the sixties had been a wraparound, environmental reinforcement. Wearing long hair had been like being part of a ubiquitous and generally benevolent family. When we saw each other, there was a sense of wearing our hearts on our sleeves. There was a lot of color on everybody. It was lovely in many ways.

These were dramatic, sometimes hairpin turns that required the greatest care and precision in a car, let alone a bus, and we were moving at an astonishing speed. Was it all right?

We stopped near the top of Mount Tamalpais. An old man moved to the front of the bus and before stepping down to the road, he turned to the driver and said, "That was a beautiful ride. Thank you!"

Genius has the means to provide for what isn't as strong in others. Haydn seems to state something exactly right musically. D. H. Lawrence is sometimes the one writer of all of them to read. Black night now fallen outside, I realized what was happening was pure, unforetold wonder, and for a moment the tension in me broke.

AMERICA: MEDITATIONS IN AN EMERGENCY

Hegemony ... is fundamentally a process of education carried on through various institutions of civil society in order to make normative, inevitable, even "natural" the ruling ideas of ruling interests. The hegemonic process is a way of gaining free assent ... [The] various constituents of ruling interests, especially what Gramsci would call their "traditional intellectuals," and what [Kenneth] Burke calls the various "priests" of the pulpit, schools, press, radio, popular arts, (and we add television), educate [the citizen] to feel "that he 'has a stake in' the authoritative structure that dispossesses him."

FRANK LENTRICCHIA
Criticism and Social Change

AFTER TUESDAY
AN L.A. POST-9/11 JOURNAL

THE GHETTO

TUESDAY'S DESTRUCTION of the World Trade Center twin tower buildings in Lower Manhattan by two hijacked commercial airliners full of fuel that effectively turned them into flying bombs is an event that signals a global change of such magnitude that it renders previous military and political postures obsolete. In effect, the terrorist suicide mission, including a third plane crashing into the Pentagon building in Washington, brought Vietnam and the West Bank to Manhattan and Washington.

In Vietnam, we learned that we couldn't win a guerilla war against an enemy that had nowhere to go, and so, eventually, having perpetrated, and sustained ourselves, a terrible cost in human lives, we left. We can't leave New York and Washington, and we also cannot win a war against terrorism, even if we ourselves become terrorists. You can't fight fire with fire, the old saw goes; for if we turn ourselves into fire, one way or another don't we ourselves burn? In essence, the terrible events of Tuesday morning in which thousands died, make it necessary to rethink things from the ground up.

"U.S. ATTACKED" was the banner headline on Wednesday's *New York Times*, unthinkable for so long while Europe and the Middle East and Asia and Africa lived through war after war on their homelands. We have now outlived our immunity, thousands of innocent civilians having paid with their lives. If we are to honor these dead now, can it be with more dead – with purposeful vengeance, planned and executed with the expertise of Tuesday's suicide mission?

Having taken off in Boston on cross-continental flights to Los

Angeles, two commercial airline jets were eventually piloted, presumably by the hijackers, to crash into one or the other of the twin towers. The "deep, unyielding anger" spoken of by President Bush in his address to the nation is not uncalled for, nor is his vow to bring the people responsible for this tragedy to justice. But the fact is that the people directly responsible are already dead, and is it possible that we ourselves know any more deep and unyielding anger than the perpetrators of this terrible violence, who patiently, methodically, and with great expertise according to the *Times*, executed their suicide mission?

If we can exact justice without ourselves becoming human sacrifices, perhaps there is a way to win a terrorist war, but common sense dictates that it cannot be done. If men and women anywhere are willing to die for a cause perceived to have greater value than their lives, then all bets are off, as we experienced Tuesday. The answer is not to deepen our commitment to match the fanaticism necessary to a suicide mission, unless we wish to see justice exacted at the expense of the planet itself.

Rather, we must regather our forces and go now, as one more member of a global union, to the table. We must sit down patiently, earnestly, and humbly with Israel and Palestine, with Northern Ireland, and with the citizens of all the other global flashpoints, as well as those of our own inner cities, and seek solutions that will extend human dignity and well-being more equitably among us. "We all live in the ghetto," Yoko Ono said years ago. Tuesday's eruption is the most terrible signature yet of the price we pay when we allow the ghetto to remain because it's not in our immediate environs.

BY FRIDAY

Although he is making a game try at it, President Bush doesn't seem to have much in the way of natural capacity to address the psychological and emotional shock of Tuesday's terrorist attacks on Washington and New York, and one feels a kind of queasy disorientation in this long moment, as if the country had slipped its groove.

The beginning of that sensation happened with an earlier, albeit far less powerful shock: when the Supreme Court overruled the

Florida state supreme court's decision to recount the Florida vote, and thus gave us a president by circumvention rather than by exercise of the democratic process. While this wasn't unique in our history, the Supreme Court's override in which the justices reversed their previous records in favor of states' rights, was unprecedented in its baldness. It took place in broad daylight, as it were.

An old power cadre, one steadily eroding but one tenacious in its will to not go gently into that good night, was thus able to install their candidate. George W. Bush was a man who had only in the last decade made politics his life, but one perceived to be possessed of an engaging decisiveness, a "leadership" quality, that would, it was hoped, recommend him to a politically disengaged American public. Although his opponent, Al Gore, appeared rather stolid, he was of course far better prepared to be the president. Mr. Bush behaved throughout most of the campaign as though he'd already been elected – by certain lights this was a part of his charm – and he seemed a bit peeved when in fact he didn't win. America, despite all our follies, is a wiser republic than we are often given credit for being.

There is good reason to take every precaution to avoid a repetition of Tuesday's violence against thousands of innocent civilians, but it is hard to credit the militarist cast of the administration's new goal. To strike at terrorism across the planet is to strike at a chimera that is likely to multiply with each assault it endures. Before Tuesday, the president's budget involved a revival of the Star Wars missile shield, a chimera itself according to many of our own military experts, and a defense system that even if it were to be deployed successfully would have been entirely useless in defending us against Tuesday's attack.

Is it any less chimerical to believe that terrorism can be eliminated on our planet by military means, presumably by killing all terrorists, or perhaps by making an example of certain key terrorists and frightening the others into docility – tactics historically modeled for us by terrorists themselves? At the same time, the president's call to war may go back to 1941 and the attack on Pearl Harbor, after which Roosevelt was able to rally the country to the Allied cause in Europe. If that is the paradigm, it seems mismatched to today's circumstances. We are not at war with a nation or even a military power. What the terrorists accomplished on Tuesday didn't involve conventional military weaponry at all.

THE WEEKEND

The damage of last Tuesday morning was so ghastly – I knew at least one person who died – that I'm uneasy with the sense I have of a Kali-like power in play that exceeds the particulars of the named players and the thousands of still unknown dead. I spent several years recently working in an office with sixty office mates, and my heart goes out to the anonymous dead and their families and loved ones. Many of the dead were, I believe, like my own office mates, for whom I feel abiding respect and affection. These were secretaries and mid-level managerial staff required to be at work by nine in the morning. They were ordinary working Americans summoned out of life in an instant. It remains unfathomable to me what happened, and I don't expect ever to fathom it.

At the same time, as the days have passed since Tuesday's catastrophe, I've begun to see the events of that morning on the scale of a biblical parable, although, I hasten to add, not one in the mold portrayed by the religious right.

Osama bin Laden, presumably behind the attacks, must be reckoned a diabolical genius. Here is a man who without military resources managed on a single morning to render a blow to the heart of the corporate military industrial complex the power of which hasn't begun to be reckoned. The fact that the Bush administration has already proposed war seems even at this early date like a reflexive reaching back to a paradigm that bin Laden effectively damaged beyond repair. Terrorism isn't a nation state with a military to encounter, and the idea of roaming the planet to root out its adherents in every corner of the globe seems absurd.

The long-proposed missile shield called Star Wars, massively if unsuccessfully funded by Ronald Reagan and recently revived by President Bush, is surely obsolete after Tuesday morning. Even if it could be successfully deployed, it couldn't have protected us, and if it couldn't protect us, what use could it be?

Mr. Bush is a straightforward salesman for a corporate world

order, and his Vice President Mr. Cheney and Secretary of State
Colin Powell are steady proven hands in its service. This is the new
world order, as we know it, the world view also represented by ex-
President Clinton and Prime Minister Blair. These men each have
their distinctive qualities and powers, but they share fundamental
assumptions about the way the world should run with relatively
minor variations. With Tuesday's events, a great deal more than the
World Trade Center towers collapsed, but those towers were certainly an adequate symbol, as was a partially destroyed Pentagon
building. What follows is from a letter by Tamin Ansary, a native of
Afghanistan who has long resided in the United States, forwarded
to me on e-mail this morning, Saturday, September 15th:

> Bin Laden is a political criminal with a master plan. When
> you think Taliban, think Nazis. When you think bin Laden,
> think Hitler. And when you think "the people of Afghanistan"
> think "the Jews in the concentration camps." It's not only
> that the Afghan people had nothing to do with this atrocity.
> They were the first victims of the perpetrators. They would
> love for someone to eliminate the Taliban and clear out the
> rats nest of international thugs holed up in their country. I
> guarantee it.
>
> Some say, if that's the case, why don't the Afghans rise up
> and overthrow the Taliban themselves? The answer is, they're
> starved, exhausted, damaged, and incapacitated. A few years
> ago, the United Nations estimated that there are 500,000 dis-
> abled orphans in Afghanistan – a country with no economy,
> no food. Millions of Afghans are widows of the approximately
> two million men killed during the war with the Soviets. And
> the Taliban has been executing these women for being women
> and has buried some of their opponents alive in mass graves.
> The soil of Afghanistan is littered with land mines and almost
> all the farms have been destroyed. The Afghan people have
> tried to overthrow the Taliban. They haven't been able to.
>
> ... At the moment, of course, "Islam" as such does not
> exist. There are Muslims and there are Muslim countries, but
> no such political entity as Islam. Bin Laden believes that if he

can get a war started, he can constitute this entity and he'd be running it. He really believes Islam would beat the west. It might seem ridiculous, but he figures if he can polarize the world into Islam and the West, he's got a billion soldiers.

If the West wreaks a holocaust in Muslim lands, that's a billion people with nothing left to lose, even better from bin Laden's point of view. He's probably wrong about winning, in the end the West would probably overcome – whatever that would mean in such a war; but the war would last for years.

I don't have a solution. But I do believe that suffering and poverty are the soil in which terrorism grows. Bin Laden and his cohorts want to bait us into creating more such soil, so they and their kind can flourish. We can't let him do that. That's my humble opinion.

It seems unlikely that President Bush and his staff will turn in their tracks and embrace a solution that would address "suffering and poverty as the soil in which terrorism grows," even though they now face an adversary – and I would imagine a number of already-chosen successors should he be eliminated – who seems equal to the task of waging war with the corporate global hegemony. Does the average American citizen oppose ameliorating the suffering of the many in Afghanistan? I don't think so. But in the past week of talking with people, family, friends, and strangers, I've been struck by how many, including some of the best educated, seem in thrall to the very selective information purveyed by our mainstream news channels. This information in turn plays to the war sentiment being promoted by the administration, even while that sentiment plays to bin Laden's master plan, according to the letter above.

Tuesday saw successive, horrifying acts of violence against thousands of innocent civilians. What happened rivals in character if not in scale the dropping of the bombs on Hiroshima and Nagasaki. (According to Gore Vidal in *The Last Empire*, Truman knew well before he ordered the dropping of the bombs that the Japanese were ready to surrender but chose to do it to frighten Stalin.) Uniquely, in this week's carnage, one seems to catch a glimpse of the destroyer, the death goddess Kali, or whatever name one might care to give it, flashing between the repetitive pulsations of our news media. This is movement, an eruption such as I never thought I'd witness in my lifetime. The American presidential election of 2000 showed us how far the power structure was willing to go to get the outcome it wanted, and as Americans we live in the shadow of a corporate lockdown that has effectively rendered us a mere outpost in a high-stakes global game. On Tuesday an evil hydra-headed countermeasure struck with a precision and speed one couldn't imagine before it happened.

RUSSIAN LESSONS

Joseph Stalin was the terrorist who dominated the last century, hewing to power as the leader of the Russian Soviet state and its satellite countries for decades. That he arose out of the hopes of the Russian Revolution, the seeds of which had germinated in the writings of European thinkers and historians for centuries, and the idea of which was to lead the mass of humankind to a better life, is the irony that can attend the outcome of a revolution.

If one studies Stalin's Soviet state, an extraordinary picture of a society in a kind of sustained contortion emerges. The fact that that same society produced perhaps the greatest poets of the century is a kind of miracle, and the writings and recorded statements of Boris Pasternak, Anna Akhmatova, Osip Mandelstam, and Marina Tsvetaeva are a practical college of information about how terrorism operates.

At one point in his writings, Mandelstam refers to "nostalgia for the present," as if the murderous tyranny that Stalin presided over simply eliminated the pleasures and beauties to be found in the moment. If one was afraid that the Soviet secret police, Stalin's interior army, would knock on one's door at any time of the day or night and one would be arrested and taken away to be imprisoned or murdered, or that this would happen to one's wife or child, it was difficult to remember to smell the roses, to breathe in the spring air, or to take delight in newly fallen snow.

In his novel *Doctor Zhivago*, written during the Stalinist epoch, Pasternak went back to a prerevolutionary period in which there was a chaotic, unsettled feeling in the air that eventually led to the revolution. Much of the novel portrays the earlier period, a psychological springtime of possibilities that was eventually displaced by the social lockdown that Pasternak endured as he wrote it. *Doctor Zhivago* is a love story and one of the most extraordinary evocations of the beauties of nature ever written.

For others of the Russian citizenry, maintaining the connection with the here and now was even more difficult. When one is under threat of irrational murder – and Stalin seemed to issue execution orders on whim, eventually accounting for millions upon millions of lost lives – the gravest ill, short of murder, may be the power of the terrorist to duplicate his own state of mind in those he terrorizes. A kind of psychological cloning can occur as the threat to one's life, and the lives of those one loves, increasingly dominates and ultimately preempts normal life.

The Russian populace of those years was, it sometimes seems, collectively looking over its shoulder to catch the approach of the terrorist and avoid it. Avoiding it might also involve catching one's neighbor in an act that might provoke Stalin – and given Stalin's instability, such provocation might be found almost at will. If one failed to report a betrayal, one might, in turn, also provoke the leader. In effect, the terrorist passed his own mindset on to his victims: his paranoia on the one hand and his cruelty on the other.

"Only someone who has listened to the radio in Russia for the last twenty-five years really understands Communism," the indomitably witty Anna Akhmatova once commented. And then there is this celebrated poem by Marina Tsvetaeva (translated by Elaine Feinstein):

> I know the truth – give up all other truths!
> No need for people anywhere on earth to struggle.
> Look – it is evening, look, it is nearly night:
> *what* do you speak of, poets, lovers, generals?
>
> The wind is level now, the earth is wet with dew,
> the storm of stars in the sky will turn to quiet.

And soon all of us will sleep under the earth, we
who never let each other sleep above it.

With the terrorist attack on New York and Washington on September 11, America was abruptly initiated into a new, unprecedented era of its history. There are many ways in which the experience of those in Russia under Stalin isn't comparable. But the power of the terrorist to duplicate his mindset is one that may remain applicable now: whether it involves mirroring the violence, the anger, or the hatred. The answer of the poets was to do all they could to remain in touch with the present moment, to maintain their love of life itself.

September 12–16, 2001

AFTER TWO WEEKS

AFTER TWO WEEKS

LOS ANGELES (September 26, 2001) Two weeks having passed
since the terrorist attack on New York and Washington, one senses
that there are fundamental problems in the way the Bush administration is addressing the crisis. On the one hand, it seems that cooler
heads than the president's have prevailed regarding reprisal. This
isn't a military enemy and doesn't encompass a known target. So far
Afghanistan hasn't been bombed, which would be a show of force
likely to kill innocent civilians. If it can be called a war, this is a war
without borders, largely faceless, and when and where the next terrorist strike may occur nobody knows. Airport security has been
augmented and rethought. Attorney General Ashcroft is warning
now of a possible outbreak of chemical warfare – leakage of poison
gas from a truck after a suicide mission on the highway, poison gas
in the ventilation system of a skyscraper, among other scenarios.
Such terrorist tactics are now a part of the daily thoughts of perhaps
a majority of Americans, and this is an unprecedented change that
has occurred since the events of September 11th. Los Angeles still
seems less crowded at its restaurants and bookstores than it was
before the attack. Many people still apparently feel safer at home.

President Bush looks insecure, and one can feel sympathy for
a man who seems out of his depth. At the same time, he seems un-
willing or unable to draw on the resources available to him as
commander-in-chief. Where are Bill Clinton, Jimmy Carter, and
Jesse Jackson? These are international figures who might serve the
country now, but Bush's difficulties filling his office may keep him
from calling on help from anyone who might unwittingly call attention to his uncertain bearing as president. In contrast, in New York,
while Mayor Giuliani is the central figure, he is supported by Gov-

ernor Pataki, and Senators Schumer and Hillary Clinton, all of whom have bonded across partisan lines to meet the crisis.

It is past time to convene an international tribunal to study the root causes of terrorism, surely as vital a step as calling for international military coalitions, resources, and strategies. This problem is not going to go away with our determination to raise our security standards and bring a visible military presence to the East. Clearly, though, what should happen now doesn't jibe with the business of business.

The unspoken issue is what is at stake for the multinational corporations who are the *de facto* global leadership. One senses that retaliation has been deferred because it would only further destabilize world markets and the infrastructure upon which they are based. But CEOs are not known to be open to addressing actual realignment of power, resources, and wealth in the name of peace and order, vital though that may be for our future. The idea seems to be to advance every idea of containment and defer addressing causes indefinitely.

This virtually guarantees another episode of terrorism, but like global warming, it may be allowed to occur. This kind of myopia has long been the accepted if undeclared business outlook, despite the advancing threat of a planetary biohazard. Will it change now with the more immediate threat of terrorism? Part of the problem is that the people the president ultimately answers to are as invisible as the terrorists.

Star Wars Rides Again

While he may not rationally comprehend the world we see before us, Ronald Reagan has lived, as of Sunday, October 7th, into a time in which the mindset that he nurtured and believed in is back with a vengeance. While cutting so-called entitlement programs across the board – the free lunch programs for poorer children at public schools, for instance – President Reagan spent billions of dollars developing the Star Wars Missile Shield, in the belief that it would guard us against any and all incursions on our democratic freedoms.

In fact President Bush, just before the September 11th terrorist strikes, was trying to revive the defunct Star Wars program, which had finally been declared an impossible undertaking and dropped from the military budget. One significant lesson of the tragedy on that Tuesday morning less than a month ago, was that Star Wars – had it been effectively deployed – would have availed nothing in deterring the attacks. Well, one *thought* it was a significant lesson.

Millions of terrified Afghan civilians are on the move, it was reported on Sunday. These bomb and missile attacks are not as site-specific and small in scope as initially they were promoted to be, but a thunderous orchestration of the greatest military power the world has ever known against a country without a military, with millions of innocent men, women, and children traumatized in the midst of it.

The idea of the mission, of course, is the same as the idea initially behind Star Wars. It will protect us against incursions against us, in this case by the terrorist enemy Osama bin Laden and his followers.

But the people who flew the planes into the World Trade Center towers and the Pentagon didn't live in Afghanistan. They lived in apartment buildings in Florida, Boston, and New York. What we did on Sunday, with the support of British missiles fired from their submarines, was to fan the international flames of terrorism. It's the equivalent of setting a terrorist minefield across the planet. The attack on Sunday set terrorist timers ticking in God knows how many places.

Over the days and weeks succeeding the attacks, our major newspapers began to publish detailed stories on the events of the preceding day in the international theater of the fight against terrorism. Even a casual perusal of the newspaper each morning yielded page after page that included photographs of men with dark skin, frequently with heavy beards, wearing robes, with fezzes or turbans on their heads, on occasion riding camels. Abruptly, a different part of the globe was the central focus of our newspapers. We could now study these figures and learn what they said and thought. If we are truly a global civilization today, such information was not only important but vital.

However, the Star Wars mindset has nothing to do with that small heartening sign of a broadening awareness of the larger planet. Rather it was nurtured in an idea of America as a safe haven that could be guarded against any and all who had disagreements with us.

The Bush administration bombed Afghanistan as if September 11 never happened, implementing a powerful show of force in an outmoded, indeed counterindicated military paradigm. At the same time, it proceeded in essence oblivious to the millions of innocent lives affected – some of them surely ended – by this mindless exercise.

WORLD WAR III

The ongoing bombing of Afghanistan and the concurrent incidence of anthrax exposure in the offices of ABC, CBS, and NBC, and in Governor Pataki's office in New York and Senate Majority Leader Tom Daschle's office in Washington, comprise what could be perceived as World War III. "We will not be terrorized," President Bush said Wednesday on his way to China. But the comment only underscored the administration's failure to deal with what after only a month has already changed the lives of most Americans.

Given the incongruity of bombing a country ravaged by earlier bombing by the Russians, with a native population undergoing mass starvation, while at the same time envelopes with American postmarks arrive at the headquarters of our government and media containing "weapon grade" anthrax, the war seems to be proceeding on two different tracks, in two languages without the benefit of a translator, and even in two historical time zones. The United States enacts an expensive but outmoded military stratagem on a people who are already helpless and starving, and terrorists operate with chilling precision to effectively dismantle our government and economy while utilizing our own 34-cent stamps. We will bomb Afghanistan back to the Stone Age, we say, perhaps because our military strategists desperately need some company there.

So we remain stuck in an untenable position, notwithstanding all tough talk to the contrary. Racism is a part of it – we don't like to be told to change our policies by people who dress differently than we do and have dark skin. But isn't this more than racism? It's as if the Bush administration, in its unbudging conviction that there can be no credible argument with our position in the Middle East and Central Asia, regards the terrorists as a subspecies – as some sort of

Darwinian sport that must be stamped out of the gene pool. One remembers that before the September 11th attacks, the people fighting against corporate violation of the environment had been christened, without a hint of irony, "ecoterrorists."

The question is how do we come out from under such leadership? While the sleep patterns of Americans are being affected and people gorge on comfort food and "apocalyptic sex," our president continues to appear in photo opportunities with primary school children, and it may be time for him to start listening to his favorite companions. Every school child knows that killing innocent people is wrong, and it doesn't make you popular. American children also know that the color of a person's skin isn't important.

It's disheartening to hear public figures, grown-ups, calling their fellow human beings evil as if we ourselves knew some kind of impunity to the phenomenon. While children believe in good and evil as inexorably separate, isn't part of the passage into adulthood comprised in the recognition that the two are in each of us, and one or the other can get the upper hand on a moment's notice? Perhaps only certain of the very rich continue to believe that evil is something that only exists outside them. But as F. Scott Fitzgerald once told us, "The very rich are different from you and me."

THE PATRIARCHY

The problem with the patriarchy currently at home in the executive branch of our government is that like most patriarchies, it's not very fast on its feet. On September 11th it was hit by a wall we call terrorism, and a month later it's bashing its head against that wall as an agreed-upon strategy. The thinking seems to be that if we prove we can hit this wall over and over again, after a while it won't be there anymore. What is actually called for is that our leadership take a step back from the wall so that it can be seen for what it is and henceforth stop bashing its head against it.

"I don't have anthrax," President Bush told reporters last week. When asked if he'd been tested, he declared more vehemently, "I don't have anthrax." That's the patriarchy. You don't ask the

patriarchy to answer questions about its own well-being because
that would imply vulnerability, and the patriarchy can't allow for
that, because if it did, it wouldn't be the patriarchy anymore. It
would be another mortal being in the midst of a very difficult time.

The patriarchy, inevitably, leads to the infantilizing of its citizenry, because when there's a father figure calling the shots, we can
snuggle up with CNN or *Survivor* secure in the knowledge that our
leaders are at the helm, weathering the storm for us. The problem
is that's not what's happening. The leaders are trying to act cool,
calm, and collected – Dick Cheney and Colin Powell are marvels of
easy discourse no matter what they're actually saying – but the reality is, day in and day out, they're banging their heads – and ours –
against a wall.

We need to ask the question that the former KPFK host Laura
Flanders said last week at Skylight Books was on everybody's lips
when she stepped outside her apartment building and onto the street
in Manhattan not far from the World Trade Center that morning of
September 11th. The question everyone was asking, Flanders said,
was *Why?* Why would people hate us so much that they would com-
mit this horrific crime against humanity?

"A monstrous eruption of truth," Susan Sontag in *The New Yorker*
called the events of that morning, and has been much excoriated for
it ever since. Bill Maher was warned by his bosses, who were warned
by our executive branch, that he needed to watch his mouth after he
declared on *Politically Incorrect* that the terrorists who had committed the suicide missions weren't cowards. It's hard not to accept
the truth of what he said, except that it contradicted the position of
the patriarchy.

Our country is in the amount of trouble we are in right now, one
might surmise, because our leaders would rather sustain the patriarchy – and its extensions into the countries and their economies
that breed the terrorists – than accept that we must share this planet
with our fellow beings; that it would make sense, for instance, to
address the problem that millions of them are not fed, clothed, and
sheltered to any minimum standard of decency. What the truth of
September 11th seems to be about is that the third world would like

to be part of the first world, and for a variety of reasons, the patriarchy is not eager for that to happen.

The fact is, though, it has happened, and nothing the patriarchy
can do can change that. That it happened, however, doesn't seem to
register with the patriarchy. No more than, say, global warming reg-
isters. We know global warming is occurring – the planet is getting
measurably warmer because of the lifestyle engendered by the corporate global hegemony – but the patriarchy dismisses that as a
small matter, not genuinely important.

The economy is a shadow of its former self, and not just our economy, the global economy. Why? Because the world changed overnight, but the global leadership remains impervious to the meanings
behind the change. These folks aren't thinking clearly, one might
say, but someone else might answer that they never have before, and
that never seemed to matter much.

So what is to be done while the global corporate military-indus-
trial complex holds on to some chimerical notion of containment of
terrorism without acknowledging any legitimacy to its sources, reasons, and goals? I don't know and admit finding the daily news dis-
tressing enough to give it only the barest once-over each morning.
But something else keeps coming back to me – something I saw in
an ad printed in the newspaper one morning recently. It was a quote
from Gandhi. He said, "When I despair, I remember that all through
history the way of truth and love has always won. There have been
tyrants and murderers and for a time they seem invincible, but in
the end, they always fall – think of it, ALWAYS."

This gives me comfort, but not because it suggests a way out of
our deadly face-off. What I get out of Gandhi's words is that they
suggest that the universe is some kind of thinking reed of its own,
with its own evolutionary trajectory. So that even if we all go down
with this particular ship, with this particular patriarchy holding us
in lockdown, the sun will come out again over the disaster, the bit-
ter lesson, and whatever or whoever is left will pick up the pieces
and go on.

OUR AMERICA:
MEDITATIONS IN AN
EMERGENCY

CONSUMER EDUCATION

DURING THE SIXTIES, there was a sentiment abroad to the effect that college, while leading to a degree that would be useful in pursuing employment, might not necessarily strengthen one's mind. Absorbing information, it was perceived, wasn't necessarily a corollary to ideation.

Russell Jacoby's *The Last Intellectuals: American Culture in the Age of Academe* includes a clear-eyed review of the strange turns in the road in the odyssey of intellectuals who came of age during the sixties, many of whom now hold tenured positions at universities. Where is the Edmund Wilson of this radical generation or the Lewis Mumford? Jacoby asks. Where, that is, is today's left-liberal generalist who writes for the common reader? Jacoby has a number of interesting answers, but perhaps the central one has to do with the necessity of not making waves within the routinely choppy waters of academe if one wants to stay on. Evidently the New Left intellectual learned that he could settle into the middle class by exercising a certain discretion in the matter of voicing his views, an option that might incidentally comprise making those views virtual gibberish to the common reader.

Jacoby is less appreciative of literary writers than one might wish. He dismisses Lionel Trilling for his fuzzy political thinking and misses that the circumlocutions of Trilling's best writing (*Sincerity and Authenticity,* for instance) remind one of Casals buzzing like a bee over a transcript by Bach. He is coolly hilarious, however, when he reviews some of the jargon-studded and effectively unreadable treatises that our revolutionary brothers have cooked up inside the university system. Here is Richard Sennett (1943–), a New York University professor, in his book *Authority*:

> These, then, are five ways to disrupt the chain of command, all based on the right and the power to review through discussion decisions which come from higher up: the use of the active voice; discussion of categorization; permitting a variety of obedience responses to a directive; role exchange; face-to-face negotiation about nurturance. These disruptions are opportunities to connect abstract economic and bureaucratic forces in human terms. . . And it is by these disruptions that the fear of omnipotent authority might be realistically lessened.

Jacoby also alludes to the failure of the left liberal journals to nurture young writers. Most of the regular contributors to *The New York Review of Books*, for instance, are either now in their sixties or older or English imports, whereas neoconservative journals like *Commentary*, *The New Criterion* and *The American Scholar* have judiciously cultivated a younger crop of writers.

Remember debating teams in high school? There was a certain sort of student, clear-eyed and possessed of good diction, who excelled at these contests, projecting both intelligence and idealism. What's really needed in our national dialogue these days, I think, is a figure who echoes that exemplary high school debater: a plainspoken idealist unafraid to call things by their rightful names.

In fact, we have a number of writers who are speaking straightforwardly about what is going on, notably, again, older ones. Noam Chomsky led the way, although he can be tedious to read. A far better writer, and one who seems in synch with Chomsky and indeed praises him, is Gore Vidal. There are Chomsky and Vidal, then, and one finds older titles here and there.* *Toward a History of Needs*, by Ivan Illich, is a book from the early seventies, that interim during which the sixties were for all intents and purposes still alive. The

---

* Among newer titles, Arundhati Roy's *Power Politics* would head my list.

book, an old paperback copy of which I came across recently, speaks about what Illich calls "the modernization of poverty."

An important aspect of that modernization is psychological rather than fiscal. Illich talks about the way education has become a process whereby a few receive expert status, by formal degree or certification, and, lacking that credential, the rest of us are officially disempowered. It's as if the fact that someone is formally certified makes it necessary for the rest of us to stop thinking or even using common sense in the area of our neighbor's expertise. This is good for capitalism, of course, where a financial premium can now be exacted for the expertise, but bad for the populace at large. One is reminded of the stock market surges these days with the announcements of major layoffs.

For centuries, women gave birth in their homes or outside of them in nature. Nowadays in Western society, most women give birth in hospitals, often under sedation or, far worse, compelled to submit to an unnecessary C-section. Then too, the pro-choice bumper sticker that declares "Your Religion Ends Where My Body Begins" signals a societal split. The motives behind the conservative position on abortion are complex. Intertwined as they are with capitalist patriarchy, they comprise a kind of right-wing double-helix – and within this ideological scheme, it would be natural that male-dominated institutions would determine how a woman should deal with a pregnancy, rather than the woman herself.

At the other end of the life cycle, people used to die in their homes or just outside of them in nature. Today a person is likely to die in a hospital while a spectrum of medical strategies is utilized to prolong his or her life – unless the proper papers have been rigorously executed to forbid it. Dr. Kevorkian, a brave man, is in prison on behalf of the right of the terminally ill and dying to decide whether or not they wish to end their lives.

ALL THE NEWS THAT FITS

The American media likes a good story, but what it perceives that story to be, in any given instance, may leave a lot of questions begging. The coverage of the 2000 presidential campaign often seemed to focus on fluctuations in the polls rather than substantive issues, and at best there was only cursory attention afforded the Nader campaign, perhaps on the basis of the poor prognosis for third-party challenges in the polls. This is the equivalent of covering numbers rather than ideas, and if one thinks of politics as something other than a sporting event, such coverage comprises implicit censorship. The press covering the polls isn't really a story. It's a printout with captions.

In a different arena, some years ago the writer Jeffrey Masson sued the writer Janet Malcolm of *The New Yorker* for libel in response to a profile Malcolm wrote of Masson for the magazine. In the coverage that I read of the case, there was little if any mention of the substantive issue involved. There have been various decisions and appeals over the years in the case and a final determination may still be to come, but a thorough elucidation of its substance seems less and less likely as the years go by.

Several decades ago, Jeffrey Masson was a star in the notably testy psychoanalytic firmament and managed to become the director of the Sigmund Freud Archives, to which access was virtually non-existent before his advent. Given access, Masson created a major controversy in psychoanalytic circles by declaring that the father of psychoanalysis had suppressed information contained in notes he had taken which had been preserved in the archives. According to the notes, said Masson, many of Freud's female patients for hysteria had been sexually molested by their fathers. Freud's public position on the issue had been that these patients only *fantasized* relations with their fathers, his Electra complex counterpart to the Oedipus complex.

Again the press saw the lawsuit as the equivalent of a sporting event, the primary issue being who would win. What was Masson's evidence? And Janet Malcolm's evidence in her profile that contradicted his conclusions? We didn't hear much of either from *The New York Times*, and yet the real significance of the story, it seems self-evident, has to do with the issue in dispute. If Freud decided, for whatever reason, to suppress the historical record of a significant number of his female patients, that historical record could now be altered or significantly augmented, and we would learn more about the Victorian society in which psychoanalysis was born.*

Another story involves the lawsuit Lillian Hellman initiated against Mary McCarthy near the end of both their lives. The immediate impetus for the legal action was McCarthy's reply to Dick Cavett on his talk show when he asked McCarthy what she thought of Lillian Hellman.

"Every word she writes is a lie," McCarthy answered, "including 'and' and 'the.'"

One imagines the elderly but regal Hellman reaching for her telephone to call her attorney upon hearing these words. Hellman was then a very wealthy woman and in any case never one to be trifled with. McCarthy, though comfortable, wasn't wealthy. Sadly, the last years of both of these distinguished American writers' lives were in part occupied with their legal dispute.

Why did McCarthy, in old age, react as intemperately as she did, prompting Hellman to strike back with equal force, legal guns blazing? It would be in the nature of a happy accident if one found out much in the media coverage of the dispute. What had happened, we were told, was that McCarthy called Hellman a liar, and that prompted the law suit. To anyone with a more than glancing familiarity with the two writers, it was clear that the source of the trouble ran back in time and had historical as well as literary significance.

It was about Stalinism. McCarthy had been an important part of the group of leftist intellectuals of the thirties who broke away from the Communist party in *Partisan Review* when word of Stalin's murderous regime in Russia first surfaced. Hellman and her friend Dashiel Hammett discounted that news for a longer time, in the hope, no doubt, that it had been exaggerated, and, perhaps, that there might even be some mitigating rationale in the effort, initiated with the Russian Revolution, to bring forward a more equitable economic system.

---

* When I eventually read Masson's *The Assault on Truth*, the book in which he documents his case, it proved to be far less substantive than I'd imagined – in effect a tempest in a teapot.

That Lillian Hellman in her celebrated memoirs, including *Pentimento* and *Scoundrel Time*, portrayed herself and Dashiel Hammett so winningly that they emerged as latter-day American folk heroes, must have irked McCarthy, whose later career as a writer knew no such efflorescence. Then too, how deep the grudges of the thirties leftist factions ran is a story that remains to be told. One would like a history of the various gradations between Stalinism and Leninism, among Trotskyite and Fellow Traveler, Popular Front and Henry Wallace supporter, written for the common reader. In fact, the lawsuit itself might have been, and still might be, an opportunity to tell the story. The ball wasn't dropped by the press here; it was never picked up.

The result of this kind of journalism is a degree of foreshortening of the public's historical memory that amounts to a sort of institutionally enforced amnesia. This is advantageous only to those who would like a public with no historical memory. And what group would that be, one might wonder.

The recent merging of the news and advertising departments of a major newspaper like the *Los Angeles Times* suggests an answer. The advertisers, who foot much of the bill for the daily publication of the *Times*, have an implicit, if unspoken and perhaps not altogether conscious interest in a socially and politically disengaged public, if only because such a public is more likely to respond impulsively to the ads in the newspaper.

Our country is a curious experiment configuring on the one hand the rhetoric of its founding charters, the Constitution and the Bill of Rights among them, and on the other the reality of its political and economic life. In short, the egalitarian principles spoken of in our charter documents are not supported by the business of business. There is a point of intersection between commerce on the one hand and public welfare on the other after which the two proceed on widely divergent paths, and, after all, it's only common sense that this be so.

If an automobile manufacturer discovers it has a hit in its sport utility vehicle line, the public welfare be damned, the manufacturer is going to be moving SUVs. The fact that drivers of smaller vehicles can't see the traffic pattern clearly around these behemoths, that the drivers of SUVs can't see much when they back up, that the popularity of SUVs have rendered most of the spaces in public parking facilities too small for adjacent vehicles, that SUVs are gas guzzlers and major polluters – all of that is as nothing when viewed in light of the bottom line.

Another example is American medicine. From a strictly market perspective, the ideal situation is a population that is ill but not dead, since both health and death eliminate the medical customer. If that seems an exaggeration, consider that we now have what is effectively a generation on various kinds of medications. Indeed, there is now a medicine for virtually everything, but one hears little about those vaunted restorers of half a century ago: plenty of rest and lots of liquids, which in those long-gone days often seemed to do the trick.

Our public airwaves are in theory owned by the American citizenry at large. In truth, during the infancy of the radio and television industries, Congress cut backroom deals with the future moguls of the broadcasting networks and in essence privatized the airwaves for profit. The same is going on now with digital bandwidths. A result is that news, per se, involves a careful sidestepping of material that involves such an understanding, the kind of lie that can be poisonous, like a glitch in what might be called the nervous system of democracy. What is the effect of a lie at the inception of a public trust? In the end it seems possible that the exact nature of the lie is forgotten, but an underlying reflex is instilled that involves stepping back from scrutiny past a certain rather superficial threshold – as if not to rattle the skeleton in the closet.

THE POWER ELITE

I found *Individualism: Old and New* by the American philosopher and educator John Dewey at a library sale. The book was originally published in 1930, the year Dewey retired as a professor at Columbia University, but my copy is a 1962 paperback reprint, a little book with big type, which I first started to read on the Stairmaster at the gym. But after my second session with it there, I brought it home and continued reading and, with a pencil in reach, started to mark certain passages.

Dewey is describing a society that is utilizing technological advances entirely in the interest of achieving financial profits, and it's a measure of the tonic breadth of his analysis that he finds the same impoverishment and dissatisfaction in the lives of the kings of industry as in the lives of the citizen-workers upon whom their wealth depends:

> Assured and integrated individuality is the product of definite social relationships and publicly acknowledged functions. Judged by this standard, even those who seem to be in control, and to carry the expression of their special individual abilities to a high pitch, are submerged. They may be captains of finance and industry, but until there is some consensus of belief as to the meaning of finance and industry in civilization as a whole, they cannot be captains of their own souls – their beliefs and aims.

In the next passage he might be characterizing the members of the World Trade Organization (WTO), who meet now in evermore remote corners of the world:

> They exercise leadership surreptitiously and, as it were, absent-mindedly. They lead, but it is under cover of impersonal and socially undirected economic forces. Their reward is found not in what they do, in their social office and function, but in a deflection of social consequences to private gain.

To which he adds, for the edification of anyone who has puzzled over the absurdly inflated salary of today's corporate CEO:

> [T]he absence of a sense of social value is made up for by an exacerbated acceleration of the activities that increase private advantage and power.

"One cannot look into the inner consciousness of his fellows," Dewey adds temperately, "but if there is any general degree of inner contentment on the part of those who form our pecuniary oligarchy, the evidence is sadly lacking."

The book's premise is that the technological revolution isn't subject to reversal, and the old romantic individualism, which variously opposed or ignored this *fait accompli*, is thus outmoded and irrelevant. The challenge, as Dewey sees it, is to address the potential of technology to change life for the better of humankind as a whole. He quotes the historian Clarence Ayres:

> Our industrial revolution began, as some historians say, with half a dozen technical improvements in the textile industry; and it took us a century to realize that anything of moment had happened to us beyond the obvious improvement of spinning and weaving.

Twenty-five years after *Individualism: Old and New*, another Columbia professor, the sociologist C. Wright Mills, atomizes in *The Power Elite* the same society Dewey addressed, which during the interim has continued on the course that Dewey had tried to warn it off. The new wrinkle that Mills elucidates is that the mind itself now is being branded, as it were, by a society in which the sole motivation and distinction is pecuniary. Speaking of the necessity of corporate support for political success in America, Mills writes in his concluding chapter, "The Higher Immorality":

> [The] most important question about the campaign funds of ambitious young politicians is not whether the politicians are morally insensitive, but whether or not any young man in American politics, who has come so far so fast, could very well have done so today without possessing or acquiring a somewhat blunted moral sensibility.

Noting a time when our statesmen and our intellectuals were often one and the same, Mills quotes John Adams: "[I]f one who was inferior is raised to be superior, unless it be by fixed laws, whose evident policy and necessity may take away disgrace, nothing but war, carnage and vengeance has ever been the usual consequence of it. . ." – which doesn't seem an unfair description of the planetary strife we have today, not yet two years along in the administration of George W. Bush.

One of the problems of our corporate-ruled planet is that enduring value of the kind these books both consider and embody is plainly at odds with the powers-that-be. Buzzwords and bugaboos like "socialism" and "card-carrying liberal" masquerade as social and political distinctions when in fact they are no more than public relations ploys to defer thought of any kind. Much that might reward and inform us in our lives is thereby marginalized.

Today, fifty years after Mills wrote, if you go to the AOL Time Warner portal, for instance, you are likely to find a single news headline – usually about terrorism or a sensational crime – and then several more story links. On the other side of the web page, given the lion's share of the space, is a celebrity update or puff piece: Gwyneth, Julia, Brad, or George. In the concluding pages of his book, Mills writes:

> Professional celebrities and . . . politicians are the most visible figures of the system; in fact, together they tend to monopolize the communicated or public scene that is visible to the members of the mass society, and thus to obscure and to distract attention from the power elite.

Who, then, is this elusive figure who appears oblivious to the carnage and suffering across the planet? Someone, we might surmise, for whom the well-being of his fellows is, at best, a peripheral question. The image might be Narcissus peering into the pond that is his mirror. Hypnotized, Narcissus ultimately falls into the water and drowns. But until then we can surmise that he is – if not content, at least mesmerized.

THE *politics* CIRCLE

The discovery of the Nazi death camps at the end of the Second World War, followed by America's dropping of atomic bombs on Hiroshima and Nagasaki, confirmed what a loose alliance of literary intellectuals in Europe and America, a group that included Albert Camus, Nicola Chiaromonte, Mary McCarthy, and Dwight Macdonald, had already concluded: The progressive evolution of mankind based on the Enlightenment ideal of rationality could no longer be taken on faith. For the same rational capacities that had fostered the industrial revolution, and such inventions as the railroad and the radio, had also led to the death factories and a mushroom cloud that would henceforth cast a shadow over all humankind.

"War and progress are obsolete," Dwight Macdonald declared in a 1945 essay in his magazine *politics*, a house organ for the group, which tended more toward anarcho-pacifism than their colleagues at *Partisan Review*, who, while breaking early with Stalinist communism, continued to give allegiance to various non-Stalinist Marxist models.

Camus wrote of the war: "In the course of a few years Europe, which was several centuries ahead in knowledge, moved several centuries ahead in moral knowledge."

At the heart of the advance in moral knowledge, according to Camus, was the realization that the monolithic models of government represented by Fascism, Nazism, Communism, and, yes, Capitalism, were simply too big and unwieldy, possessed of too much unpredictable and not uncommonly murderous power, to serve the great majority of people on the planet.

While the American philosopher-educator John Dewey would look for an evolution in consciousness to keep pace with the advance of technology, figures like Camus and Simone Weil, natives of war-ravaged Europe, called for a radical downsizing in the model of a workable society.

In his book *Dwight Macdonald and the* politics *Circle*, Gregory D. Sumner writes that Macdonald would not allow the atomic bomb to be dismissed "as an emergency expedient, a tragically necessary scientific aberration. Instead it was a representative product of industrial culture, 'as easy, normal and unforced an expression of the American Way of Life as electric iceboxes, banana splits, and hydromatic automobiles.'"

How was the world to reckon with such power, born of man's rational capacity yet leading to murder on an unprecedented scale? These writers looked back to the social vivacity of the small Greek city-state, the polis, and also found a possible prototype in the various resistance movements in Europe during the war. It would be based on behavioral modes that seemed at that moment in history all but extinct: friendship, meaningful work, social responsibility, reflection, leisure time, and an implicit willingness to forgo the most powerful new automobile, to take one instance of celebrated "progress," with the understanding that such an artifact, while it would provide a bonanza for the economic machine, didn't necessarily address deeper or more pressing needs.

In grade school, when anarchy was discussed, a traffic intersection was regularly evoked. We were asked to imagine what would happen if there were no traffic lights, no stop signs, and worst of all, no laws to punish people for vehicular misdeeds. Like clockwork, my own mind summoned up a scene of automotive wreckage and mayhem. My only firsthand knowledge of driving was the Dodge'em car ride at amusement parks, where one commandeered one's car for multiple (thrilling) crashes into other cars. It was a very long time before it occurred to me that most people would stop short of destroying their neighbor's car at the intersection if only because their own car would be destroyed at the same time.

Nowadays it seems oddly apt that the automobile became the litmus test. Here was a machine that could be commanded by the average citizen but comprised far more power than the citizen himself. In microcosm, this is the reality that so chastened the *politics* group. Could man master his own inventions? They had seen firsthand in Europe that the industrial revolution was as potent a force for evil as it could be for good.

Today we see an American president and his administration staring Narcissus-like into a pool that gives back a promise of unprecedented planetary power. Meanwhile, great numbers of American citizens, and the large majority of citizens across the globe, wonder where this might end. The *politics* group would have allowed Narcissus his suicidal folly at the pool. But they were frightened about the same man given access to power that would allow him to condemn countless others in his self-amazed trance. If that was progress, they wanted out, opting instead for a society that would keep things to human scale. Sadly, they are largely forgotten today, when we badly need a dose of their common sense.

NOTES AND COMMENTS
1974–1986

THE DRIVER: REFLECTIONS ON JACK KEROUAC

THE DRIVER GUIDES his machine through time and space faster than he could move himself. His speed is the result of the machine's power, his course a matter of his own decision, or reflex, as he goes. The slightest inaccuracy, the briefest inattention, can cost him his life – and there is also the possibility it can make him a murderer.

Having been a New Yorker from early adolescence, I got my license relatively late in life. I was twenty-eight years old, and the fact that I'd been able to break with my own pattern of so long and learn at least some fundamental skill at handling a car made me feel good.

Having gotten my driver's license, and my first car, within a few months I totaled the vehicle in an accident that might have killed me but from which I miraculously emerged unscratched. My feeling at the time was not that I had cheated death, or any such exhilaration. I felt like a very foolish, very young man – very lucky to be alive.

That accident vividly brought home to me the difference between myself and the car. The car could kill me almost casually, while for me to kill myself would involve some basic effort – outside of the car, that is. To be arrogant on the sidewalk is one thing, to be arrogant in the car something else again. A driver must be quickened to his deepest insides to the ever-changing saga the road presents to him.

Jack Kerouac's classic book *On the Road* made a hero of the driver, Dean Moriarty, based on his friend Neal Cassady, and anyone who reads it can see Kerouac's love and respect for this man and his sense of instantaneous mastery behind the wheel.

* * *

In the spring of 1967, some five years before I learned to drive, I rode from Cambridge, Massachusetts, with Ted Berrigan and Duncan McNaughton – Duncan at the wheel – up to Lowell, Massachusetts, to interview Jack Kerouac for the *Paris Review*. We arrived during an overcast afternoon at a suburban ranch house along a block of houses of the same style and got out to see who the master was.

At the time, although I'd enjoyed a number of Kerouac's books, I had no very strong feelings about him. I came along to give Ted, whose project it really was, some moral support. I knew Kerouac liked my father's writing, that in a sense his writing had followed out of the same freewheeling tradition as William Saroyan's, and I was curious to see who he was.

I don't know about Ted and Duncan, but I was most surprised by the figure we saw on the other side of the screen door. There was a stout, short guy with a potbelly in a T-shirt – a guy who looked like a construction worker who'd let himself go. His voice was a bellow. He greeted us with suspicion then started to warm after Ted introduced himself and his purpose (he had written ahead that he would be coming up), and the next thing we knew there was a scuffle going on with another body of the same approximate size and bulk that turned out to be Kerouac's Greek wife, Stella.

"No, Jackie, no!" she shouted, as she struggled with his arm at the door.

"Stella, it's Berrigan and McNaughton and Saroyan, for the *Paris Review* interview. Honest!"

Stella subsided at this, letting Jack's arm loose to open the screen door for us and subsequently proved to be a cordial hostess to a literary gathering that was more raucous than any of us might have expected. Jack was not the seasoned literary man delivering the usual well-salted tidbits of his career to the *Paris Review*. He was more like a crazy guy in a bar.

As the afternoon turned to evening – Ted had given Jack some speed, Obitrols, which he had gulped without missing a beat – and the living room darkened and no one bothered to turn on the lights, we found ourselves in the presence of a roaring nut. He had a notebook by his side and every so often would read little excerpts from it to us. At one point, after pondering a moment, he pronounced the following words out of the book and into the room as if over a PA system:

"GOY ... MEANS ... JOY."

It was amazing, and incredible, and I wondered to myself if Jack Kerouac could really be an anti-Semite (I'm half Jewish), and yet the question in the presence of this charged-up ruin of a man seemed almost irrelevant.

At one point I asked about his comment that you should let the sentence go on after you think it's said what it's supposed to – to see what images come out of it then. I referred to his book *Tristessa*, a very photographic kind of writing I thought, and asked whether he tried to see it as he was writing...

"Aw, you sound like a college composition course at Indiana University," he said.

"I know, but. . ."

"You would have liked her."

"Who?" I asked.

"Tristessa – you would have liked her. She was a beautiful little Mexican girl. . ."

I went out of that interview with a lot of crazy impressions – Kerouac standing in his dark living room in his T-shirt and bellowing some oath as he bumped the air suddenly with his belly in imitation of his father knocking a rabbi off his feet – and no ideas. In the argot of the period, my mind was blown.

Well, these past years I've done a little research, and let me make this report. Kerouac's first book was called *The Town and the City* and came out in 1950 when he was still known as John Kerouac. I made it through about half of it but couldn't finish it. It was too much like Thomas Wolfe, and there was a quality in it that bothered me, just a flicker of it here and there, but unmistakable: it was a young writer's book, and it was well done, but it had this edge of smugness. You could tell this was a guy who liked these big Thomas Wolfe-type sentences he was wielding at you, and maybe he even thought he was better than you, or better than certain characters in the book, because he wrote so well. John Kerouac – that's who that was; and if he had gone on and become successful, the interview he gave the

Paris Review would have been par for the course, the usual man of letters in his habitat. Instead of the brawl that it was.

So my guess is that John saw it all coming, saw that successful author in his future, and did a very moving and beautiful thing – threw it away. And became Jack – and followed Neal onto the road, where there was no time for pomposity – the driver could be killed or kill in one arrogant lapse on the road. His life – the life he *chose* for himself – was a very decisive action against a certain tendency of his nature, against any tendency on his part to grow smug with his gift.

So if by the time I saw him there was a middle-aged man with a beer belly in a T-shirt shouting obscenities, there was also a man utterly without the smugness of the successful writer. I know his anti-Semitism might be taken as a vicious arrogance, but I'm convinced Jack used it only as a joke on himself. Anyone who reads his books knows how much he loved Allen Ginsberg, for example. It was his particular touch of the gutter, without which maybe no real dharma bum is complete.

On a desk at the entrance of his living room – the usual ranch-house setup, carpeted, with a big TV – was in a way the most telling evidence of his own attitude toward himself. It was one of those plastic signs you see in novelty shops engraved with the words "Genius at Work." That was *Jack*. John was gone. And Jack got rid of him on the road, watching Neal drive the car.

A LETTER TO
THE NEW YORK SCHOOL

Point Arena, California
March 15, 1974

Dear Friends:

I AM WRITING this from the remote distance of Point Arena, California, and in a way the geography speaks for itself. If I was once among you, and I sometimes wonder if I ever really was, I no longer am, and it's out of a confusion of impulses that I write you now. In the past several years I've gone through the changes of marriage, fatherhood, and moving out of the city, and in the process I've not only lost touch with many of you as friends, but also have undergone a change in relation to the work you have done and continue to do, as represented in many of the periodicals that I receive as token, I guess, of our association.

What I have to say is simple, but I think it's true. In my opinion, the work being done right now by many of you who are my contemporaries is of a high quality in almost every dimension but one. Perhaps two – at least two words come to mind, but perhaps the two words are one. The two words I'm thinking of are *honesty* and *sincerity*. It seems to me that these are the two qualities most subject to abuse in the work of the New York School. I realize immediately of course that my very mention of these two words constitutes an abuse of the aesthetic with which you have now so completely identified yourselves, but I do so without really fearing the consequence. To be considered a crackpot or a cornball by the New York School would only place me with the mass of humankind in the eye of its aesthetic, and I don't mind the association at all. I only hope I'm truly worthy of it. At the age of thirty, the whole question of uniqueness becomes a little absurd – if one is alive at this age, one is inescapably among one's brothers and sisters, dependent on them for help in one form or another in simply getting through.

The point is the work I'm referring to was simply not written for humankind. It's like a machine constructed with absolutely no purpose in mind for it and immediately released on the world at large as if it were *the* gift of the ages, all rewards in itself, etc. The periodicals are bounding into the mailboxes, and there now seem to be at least three distinguishable generations at work (my own contemporaries the middle one), and yet I find it harder and harder to see the point of it all.

Even here, in this remote location, in the midst of trying to work out the purchase of some land – we are now a family of four – I received one periodical and one book in the mail today, and even before I looked through them, I knew I was the recipient of yet another exercise in utter irrelevance. As one who once considered himself in the vanguard of writing *as writing*, it is difficult for me to describe my feelings when confronted by a new generation of writers who are dedicated not to an exploration of any particular literary dimension I can identify beyond a snotty tone of voice. I know this isn't something I ever had in mind.

Beyond that, there are a number of other identifiable trends, which I would characterize briefly as: (1) Poems that prove how smart I am; (2) Poems that prove what a master of rhetoric I am; (3) Poems that prove I am a dope addict; and (4) Poems that just generally prove how hard I am to understand in any way. These are the substance of most of the periodicals I receive in the mail, and at this stage of my life it is an act of total selflessness for me to even riffle their pages, so offensive are they to my own effort and my own dream.

I am a writer because I desire to communicate with my fellow man and woman and child and writing is one avenue open to me to do this. As I experience more of life, my respect for it grows, and it is impossible for me to regard it, and anyone else in it, as the subject or object of any kind of literary exercise. It is an experience that is bigger and more profound than any telling turn of phrase or immaculate run-on sentence. It is quite simply real. Not brilliant, not arcane, not sarcastic – but alive, and in just being alive more meaning than we could ever hope to fathom. The most we could hope for, I believe, is an honest and sincere accounting of our experiences as members of this miracle of being alive in time.

I don't wish to speak for anyone here but myself, although I know what I've learned has been the knowledge of others before me as well as contemporaries. As a writer today, my goal is simple. I want to keep myself in the best physical shape I can, to develop my stamina in writing, so I can make the most of whatever small talent I may possess to tell the truth of my life as long as I live it. Just as it pleases me to give a gift to someone of anything I have made or done in sincerity, I believe it pleases life itself to live it as long and as hard and as well as one can.

I am sending this to you, in care of Bill MacKay's *Poetry Project Newsletter* of St. Mark's Church in New York, perhaps the single outlet that will reach the greatest cross-section of you, in the hopes that it will be printed. I wish you all health and happiness, and I say goodbye to you, at least for a while.

Love,
Aram (Saroyan)

CLARK COOLIDGE AND I

IN THE SPRING OF 1966, when we were both living on the same raunchy street on the Upper West Side of Manhattan, I brought out Clark Coolidge's first book, *Flag Flutter & U.S. Electric*, along with three other books, including my own *Works*, which is dedicated to Clark.

Clark's book caused an immediate stir among the poets of the New York School – Ted Berrigan, Peter Schjeldahl, Bernadette Mayer, and others – and I remember a fine reading he gave at Izzy Young's Folklore Center in the Village during which he made his poems as exciting to hear as they were on the page.

At this particular time, Clark and I were in the midst of a day-to-day dialogue about our work that was to last another year or so: we discussed everything about what we were doing and tried to offer our own senses of each other's direction.

My feeling about what Clark was doing was that he was breaking out of the normal structural patterns of language *even further* than they had already been broken out of by, say, surrealism and the current work of the New York School.

We talked about a poem that would leave no impression on the mind after it had been read: a poem with absolutely no image-track. Clark had an uncanny way of using all sorts of words and yet avoiding any kind of accumulation of these words into meaning or image.

In the mid-sixties, with the drug culture going into high gear, we felt a real concern to let the words be themselves, to avoid any "use" of words, because in using them we were avoiding a reckoning of what they were in their own reality.

We didn't want words to disappear, as they do normally in reading, into meaning or mood or whatever they might become instead of themselves.

Clark constructed galaxies, solar-systems, of nouns, verbs, adjectives, adverbs, articles and prepositions, as well as word fragments – and reading these works was, to borrow a phrase, a little like blowing in the wind.

My answer to this same problem was the one-word poem, which delivered the word stark naked, as it were, into the middle of the white expanse of the page.

The difference between the structures we employed to make what we considered almost identical statements is perhaps more telling than either of us might have guessed at the time. That is, the one-word poem eliminates the reading process entirely – it makes the word both instantaneous and continuous, like the Eternal Present.

Clark's work maintained a time element by maintaining the reading process. His work *moved*, whereas mine addressed itself to the reader in utter stop-time stillness.

Clark, that is, was taking a walk with his words, while I was, you might say, gazing at them through a microscope, stoned. Clark was more at ease with himself, I would say; I was getting stoned and looking very hard at things because I had been going too fast, I felt. I wanted my writing to slow up, and the one-word poem finally gave me the feeling that it wasn't going by too *fast*.

Clark was twenty-seven at the time; I was twenty-two.

Since that time, Clark has continued pretty much in the direction we set out in; and I have made a turnaround, writing more or less standard prose and poetry and even writing songs. What happened?

For me, I think, after I'd explored the territory for another year or two, there really wasn't much more to do. I had wiped my inner blackboard clean; and finally I had to make a new move – go up and write something on it.

I write now out of a concern with telling the truth in a very multi-dimensional time. Language to me is a medium, a kind of mirror. Time, finally, is the dimension I am most concerned with – rhythm, timing, cadence, or, to put it all in a nutshell, "voice."

Back in the sixties, we used to be so concerned about not stooping to "description" in our work, about keeping the language alive in the present, and now I find the easiest way for me to do this is to speak in my own voice, to be another member of the world we all share.

The amazing thing about Clark Coolidge is that all the time I believed he was a conceptual artist, making impersonal structures of words, he was probably in fact writing very deep, very American, very spacey autobiography, which he continues to do.

I salute him.

THE SECRET DIARIES

As *The Secret Diaries* BEGINS, in August of 1966 in New York City, Gerard Malanga, the twenty-three-year-old poet and assistant to Andy Warhol, is also becoming known for the dance he does, dressed in leather and wielding a whip, in front of the Velvet Underground, the rock band led by Lou Reed and sponsored by Warhol. With the diary's first entries, we are in the thick of Malanga's day-to-day life, a life that seems to combine in vintage sixties fashion the glamorous and the precarious in approximately equal measures. For example, Malanga doesn't have a place of his own to live at the same time that he is frequenting famous nightspots and attending big parties of the period.

He is also involved in an unhappy love affair with Susan Bottomley, a young socialite who has been given the name "International Velvet" and made a "superstar" of Warhol's underground films. For the moment, Malanga is living in Bottomley's flat at the Chelsea Hotel, but he's upset by her romantic defections to Lou Reed's apartment on the Lower East Side. At the same time, he is the object of verbal and psychological assaults from Rene Ricard, a young gay poet recently down from Boston and already becoming legendary for his wit, who seems to be in love with him.

As Malanga goes about his day-to-day duties at the Warhol "factory," as well as writing his poetry and participating in the night life at Max's Kansas City, The Arthur, and Steve Paul's The Scene, we are privileged with intimate glimpses of Lou Reed, Edie Sedgwick, Nico, Salvador Dalí, Paul Morrissey, Ingrid Superstar, Viva, and grandmaster Warhol himself. Malanga's poise in this daunting, fast-moving scene seems remarkable, especially after we learn that he earns only $1.25 an hour for his work for Warhol and with no other means of support is sometimes down to his last dollar. And one feels piquantly the twists of his romance with Bottomley.

By part two of the *Diaries*, Malanga has encountered Benedetta Barzini, the young international model and the daughter of the Italian writer Luigi Barzini. Together she and Malanga attend parties, night spots, and, dressed in identical silver outfits, a reading by Allen Ginsberg – and soon they fall in love: Malanga almost immediately, Barzini a little afterward. He is the son of Italian immigrants, raised in the Bronx; she is the daughter of the Italian intelligentsia, raised in Rome and on New York's Upper East Side. She is a highly paid model, he an all-but-penniless young poet. At the beginning of this part of the book, his attachment to Bottomley winding down, Malanga is physically and mentally playing the field, but with Barzini's appearance on the scene, there is a romantic quickening, and then as if overnight, he is involved with her to the exclusion of everyone (one might almost say every *thing*) else.

By the middle of the book, then, what started off as a vivid chronicle of a celebrated, fast-paced period and milieu begins to focus more narrowly and with increasing intensity on the diarist and Barzini. The poet now commits his thoughts with guileless romanticism, confessing among other things that he feels clean when he's with Barzini. Almost immediately, however, there appear to be obstacles to their affair from Barzini's side; and she soon seems to combine in herself the aspects of the beloved and the bitch that in the previous part of the book have been divided between Susan Bottomley and Rene Ricard.

In parts three and four, the book's second half, we are given the tortuous blow-by-blow of the unraveling of this unlikely liaison. Indeed, the diarist often seems excruciatingly masochistic to be going on at all with his effort to bring Barzini around. At the same time, in light of their differences, one can't blame Barzini for her doubts about their future together. Paradoxically, as the unhappy end of the relationship drags on, Malanga reports on the poems he is writing daily. No longer really involved with Barzini, he is nonetheless, and one might even say triumphantly, writing poem after poem for and about her while also faithfully committing each disheartening episode of their truncated romance to the diary.

Thus having begun in the swirling social vistas of high sixties Manhattan, we are now in an almost claustrophobic chamber of one young poet's mind. At a certain point, Malanga confesses that writing about Barzini is all he now has of her, and this immediately seems the real why and wherefore of the hopeless course he continues to pursue. In place of any actual reality with Barzini, he reports on his dreams of her, preternaturally vivid dreams which, if anything, seem to have greater force than what is reported from reality. In other words, by an act of mind embracing both his conscious and unconscious, the poet is re-creating her presence and holding it close. *The Secret Diaries* has by now become a chronicle of romantic obsession on the order of Maugham's *Of Human Bondage*. It also bears comparison with the *Diaries* of Cesare Pavese, the journal in which the Italian poet and novelist records his doomed love affair with the American actress Constance Dowling and which ends only a few days before Pavese's suicide.

Still, one senses the poet, who remains without an apartment and living day to day and night to night, has found in the obsessive focus of the diary a still, fixed point by which to define himself, a paradoxically "secure" frame of reference. Slowly but surely, all of churning Manhattan has fallen away, and in its place we are given an urgently transcribed meditation on an impossible love. Indeed, the words seem to be performing a sort of daily vigil until, by the diary's last entries some six months after it began, we sense that the end of this strange rite of passage is finally at hand. Near the end, too, the poet receives a copy of his first published book, *Three Poems for Benedetta Barzini*.

The Secret Diaries, along with Jim Carroll's *The Basketball Diaries* and William Burroughs Jr.'s *Speed*, seems to me a major prose testament of the sixties. Centered like the other two books in Manhattan, it achieves a gathering pitch of intensity uniquely its own. Indeed, some millennia hence, this may be *the* book to be studied for the brave candor with which it tells of the psychic turmoil and contortion known in New York City in the late hours of the twentieth century.

TEN FAVORITE BOOKS OF PHOTOGRAPHY

ANY LIST DEVOTED to favorite photography books has got to be, first of all, a study in omissions. There are so many more books that might have been on it. Having said that, I offer here a little less guiltily my top ten of the moment, in no particular order of preference:

1. *Diane Arbus* (Aperture). So much has been made of Arbus the photographer of freaks, but I wonder if we would keep going back to her photographs in books and in our minds – for her images have as great a staying power in memory as those of any photographer – if it were only a matter of midgets, nudists, transvestites, etc. She liked, for instance, twins as well, and perhaps that's a clue of sorts. I think she was going after visual *equivalents*, as it were, for a vision that encompassed more than a special, rarified world per se. "The Jewish Giant" bending kindly over his two bewildered, minuscule parents is a story of and for the generations: a visual metaphor in a medium we are taught to regard as essentially literal, especially in its documentary aspect. But if Weegee was an urban realist of a kin to, say, Zola, Arbus took photographs of the same terrain that are as remote from straightforward realism as, say, Homer.

2. *Georgia O'Keeffe: A Portrait* by Alfred Stieglitz (Metropolitan Museum of Art). This is the preeminent love affair in photography. One photograph, never before published, is taken from a vantage that makes O'Keeffe's pubic bush the dark center, her prone torso receding into the background. It has the very odor of the bed and must be among the erotic masterpieces of the medium.

3. *U.S. Camera Annual 1957*, edited by Tom Maloney (out of print). All of the *Annuals* edited by Maloney are wonderful. I choose this particular number because it was my favorite in high school. Maloney's volumes must have been a spur to Edward Steichen's *The Family of Man* exhibit and volume. They have that kind of broad humanist sweep, along with Maloney's randy and sometimes clunky eye for just about any pretty nude (especially salutary during high school). The books all seem to have a special Fifties sweetness in them, although the world they present is full of our post-war/cold-war darknesses.

4. *The Family of Man*, edited by Edward Steichen (Museum of Modern Art). A wonderful book for the whole family (haha) and very likely the best photographic anthology ever put together. Don't get fooled by deconstructionist, antihumanist babble – just look at all the pictures.

5. *Observations*, photographs by Richard Avedon, text by Truman Capote (Simon & Schuster, op). My personal favorite of Avedon's volumes, also his first, and the only one designed by his mentor, Alexey Brodovitch. This is the one where the photographer's energy is least self-conscious, most exuberant and witty. Truman Capote's text, from the period of his prime, is a perfect counterpart.

6. *Moments Preserved*, by Irving Penn (Simon & Schuster, op). Avedon and Penn are high fashion photography's answer to Picasso and Matisse: Avedon, like the Spaniard, endlessly inventive and energetic; Penn, like the Frenchman, more sensual and ruminative. His still lifes, like "Theater Accident" and "Summer Drink," are pioneering forays into a special province of photography: the arrangements artfully/artlessly contrived and then beautifully photographed in color. Unlike Avedon, Penn's highest level seems less easy to contain in book form. He is the supreme colorist of the medium. This, his first book, still comes closest I think to capturing his various powers.

7. *The Americans*, photographs by Robert Frank, introduction by Jack Kerouac (Pantheon). A photographic *On the Road* by the Swiss-

American master of the spur-of-the-moment. Coming from the most peaceful country in the world into the one most socially various and piecemeal, Frank created a moment-to-moment, semi-narrative momentum in *The Americans*. Some of these photographs must have involved tight squeezes and required courage and/or aplomb. Mary Frank, the photographer's first wife, and the couple's two young children are seen in one nighttime off-the-road shot with their faces pressed to the window of their car: looking out at the photographer they accompanied on his modern odyssey.

8. *California and the West*, photographs by Edward Weston, text by Charis Weston (Duell, Sloan and Pearce, op). Weston in a quieter key than one might expect, these photographs have a cumulative power that somehow evokes the very air of both the California desert and the agricultural valley. In the middle of the book is a photograph of Weston's young wife, Charis, who accompanied the photographer on his picture-making rounds and wrote the book's text. She sits fully clothed on a slab of stone and looks straight into the camera her husband is behind. It's one of the loveliest, sexiest portraits ever taken.

9. *Photographs and Words*, by Wright Morris (The Friends of Photography/Matrix). These photographs, which owe a debt to Walker Evans's photographs of Southern tenant farmers in *Let Us Now Praise Famous Men* (another favorite), differ from Evans's in that Wright Morris's subject is his own Nebraskan kith and kin. Hence he is able not only to enter the house but to open a kitchen or bureau drawer and photograph its contents. Morris's technique is superb, and his quiet, elegant images contain some unexpected time signatures. A drawer containing stainless steel knives and forks is papered with "Capper's Weekly" newspaper for April 25, 1939, with a photo lead, "Hitler's Army Chief," peeking over the cutlery. Morris's text, full of the novelist's understated humor, comprises a kind of autobiography.

10. *Portraits: The Photography of Carl Van Vechten* (Bobbs-Merrill, op). Van Vechten photographed famous European and American artists of the thirties, forties, and fifties – from Gertrude Stein to Billie Holliday, from Thomas Mann to Tallulah Bankhead – and his

surprisingly telling, dark-hued portraits comprise a cheering, slightly musty, somehow musical (perhaps because of all the great musicians included) succession of remarkable identities. Then too, Van Vechten seems to have photographed more of the black artists of his time than anyone else.

A few more favorites: *The Decisive Moment* by Henri Cartier-Bresson, *Eleanor* by Harry Callahan, *Tulsa* by Larry Clark, *A Way of Seeing* by Helen Levitt, and something by Brassaï.

(1986)

BACK EAST & OUT WEST
REVIEWS 1975–1976

A NEW YORK POET

Standing Still and Walking in New York. Notes and essays by Frank O'Hara. Edited by Donald Allen. Grey Fox Press: Bolinas, California. 184 pp.

IN A WAY, the original generation of the New York School of poets, in which the late Frank O'Hara figured so prominently, was like an East Coast cosmopolitan version of the Beat Generation, which came to light in the mid-fifties in San Francisco. Ironically, as O'Hara points out in a piece on Gregory Corso included in this collection, three principals of the Beat Generation – Allen Ginsberg, Jack Kerouac, and Corso himself – were all transplanted Easterners who happened to be on the West Coast when the limelight fell. But there were basic differences between these three and their counterparts at the time in New York.

O'Hara places himself most succinctly in his most famous essay, "Personism: A Manifesto," perhaps the closest thing to a definitive statement of the poetics of the New York School, when he worries if he isn't "sounding like the poor wealthy man's Allen Ginsberg. . . ." He was very nearly just that: Born the same year as Ginsberg, 1926, he was a solid, job-holding (by 1966, when he died in a freak car accident on Fire Island, he was a curator of the Museum of Modern Art), socially dexterous citizen of Manhattan at the same time that Ginsberg, with whom he had a warm friendship, was the bearded bad-boy of *Time* and *Life* notoriety. And yet in his own way, Frank O'Hara was no less intent upon the liberation of American poetry from the clutches of the New Criticism of the forties and fifties, which, as he elaborates in an interview less than a year before his death, tended to look upon art as the raw material of criticism.

Standing Still and Walking in New York is a wide-ranging collection of his notes and essays, as well as an interview with him by Edward Lucie-Smith, that completes the job begun with *The Collected Poems of Frank O'Hara* and last spring's *Art Chronicles* of rendering all of O'Hara's writing (minus his plays) back into print. It is unique in offering the poet in an informal, almost random atmosphere which, as Donald Allen states in an editor's note, allows us to see very clearly "his concerns, enthusiasms, loyalties, annoyances and distrusts."

What was O'Hara like? For one thing, he was very witty. In "Personism: A Manifesto," in which he advocates that each poem be written directly to one person, he writes, "In all modesty, I confess that it may be the death of literature as we know it. While I have certain regrets, I am still glad I got there before Alain Robbe-Grillet did." Taking to task Norman Podhoretz for his attack on the Beat Generation, "The Know-Nothing Bohemians," he calls him "a young writer who is rapidly becoming the Herman Wouk of criticism." In beginning a review of John Rechy's *City of Night*, he writes:

> The prose of John Rechy is absolutely madly involved with adverbs. Also it is full of dots and dashs and elisions, a la Kerouac, and they frequently work well to create a run-on casual, or hysterical, faggoty diction which, along with the use of capitals for Emphasis of the important feeling word (not always a noun as in German), gets marvelously accurately the Exact tone of homosexual bar-talk ... which is something, since I don't know of any other writer around who has managed this feat Unsquarely.

He is equally at home in a discussion of *Doctor Zhivago*, one of the major essays in this book, and American movie comedies of manners. He can talk about Jackson Pollock *and* Andy Warhol, about Gregory Corso *and* W. H. Auden. Throughout it all, he seems to be having a good time. More casual in tone than Allen Ginsberg, he is often equally as penetrating.

New York Times Book Review

GOODBYE TO THE 1960S

Toujours L'amour. Poems by Ron Padgett. Sun: New York. 104 pp.

The Daily Round. New poems by Phillip Lopate. Sun: New York. 85 pp.

RON PADGETT is the grand old *young* man of the New York School of poets, and it's interesting to see just what he has chosen in his antecedents to emphasize, and what he has chosen to discard. Then, too, there is the fact that Padgett came of age during the '60s, the decade in which modernism reached such a height of self-regard that it very nearly smothered itself in its own embrace. Throughout this period, Padgett could be counted on for a touch of life-affirming moderation, and a sly, going-on riotous sense of humor. Here is his "Post Publication Blues":

> My first book of poems
> has just been published.
> It is over there on the table
> lying there on the table, where
> it is lying. It has
> a beautiful cover and design.
> The publishers spent a lot of money
> on it and devoted many
> man- and woman-hours to it.
> The bookstores are ordering copies.
> Unfortunately I am a very bad poet and
> the book is no good.

Padgett operates frequently in a dimension where the seemingly calm and well-ordered movement of a text turns a corner, as if of its own volition, and the reader is put on the alert for the presence of the possibly deranged:

> It's not embarrassing to be sentimental
> When the sentiment equals
> Seeing things just as they are here now.
> It is late and in late spring with cool air and quiet
> in the room and outside in the street by the
> building I live in.
> A car goes by
> disappearing, no trace left, as if
> it entered a slit in matter and is gone forever
> with the slit then entering the slit. . . .

His method might be contrasted with Kenneth Koch's, and often John Ashbery's, in which rhetorical flourishes and idioms abound not in the service of parody but as the instrument of real and steady emotion that animates banal phrases with unexpected depth. Padgett, instead, operates at the point where the language, the thought, the emotion, discovers it has a mind and a will of its own, leaving the reader, and perhaps the writer as well, to follow its course as passive, somewhat bemused spectators. Yet this method, by emphasizing the autonomy of language, has a kind of realism of its own: pointing back to a self unencumbered by the routines and trajectories of words and grammar: a pre- or post-literate self which is the self that seems to be caught up in the mechanics of Padgett's language in something like the way Chaplin got entangled with that machine in *Modern Times*.

Phillip Lopate, another New Yorker and a contemporary of Padgett's, is handling the instabilities of modernism in another way entirely, perhaps an older way. *The Daily Round* is dedicated to Pasternak, and the title poem to Mandelstam, and the book as a whole explores the malaise of the unattached urban American – the '60s survivor who has abandoned the assumptions and liberties of that decade and taken a stand in a solitary, sober "daily round" of job, apartment, friends, and lovers. Lopate is new to me, and I found real distinction in many of these poems, or more specifically in the poet's voice, which is both the medium and the product of Lopate's concerns:

> Is the neutral state a cover for unhappiness,
> Or do I make myself impatient and unhappy
> To avoid my basic nature, which is passive and low-key?
> And if I knew the answer,
> Would it make any difference in my life?
> At bottom I feel something stubborn as ice fields,
> Like sorrow or endurance, propelling me.

After all, the exuberance of the '60s was a little wearing – every extreme seems to exact its payment – and in Lopate's poems there is evidence that the poet has found a viable alternative in accepting his own limits, as well as his own demands, for better or worse. The self is the unit upon which it all rests, an accepting, humane, realistic self; the life in it need not be extravagant in display. It is ongoing, a fact, and this is Lopate's real celebration, the life that he is simply given:

> And I am thinking:
> "Come on, you must.
> Of course live."
> That was no noble decision,
> No more than a marble
> Dropped onto the sidewalk
> Continues to roll.

This is the self that Pasternak found to be sustaining in the years of Stalinism and after. Pasternak, in effect, abandoned modernism. His final poems, written around the crisis of his being awarded the Nobel Prize, have a transcendent simplicity and clarity. I admire the way Phillip Lopate has taken this lead, and look forward to his future work.

Village Voice

PERFORMING POET

Journals and Dreams. Poems by Anne Waldman. Stonehill: New York. 211 pp.

OF ALL THE POETS of my generation, none has done more than Anne Waldman to bring poetry before the public at large. As director of Manhattan's St. Mark's Church-on-the-Bowery's Poetry Project, over the past decade she has arranged for poets from all over the globe to read in the church. During this same time she edited the church's poetry magazine, *The World*, and to date two anthologies of work that first appeared there have been issued. More recently she has emerged as an exciting reader-performer of her own poems, and has been reading her work to enthusiastic audiences throughout the country. This past summer, she and Allen Ginsberg founded the School of Poetics at the Naropa Institute in Boulder, Colorado, where she now teaches.

Journals & Dreams is her sixth volume of poems in as many years, and it is her largest. Waldman's poems are a kind of high-energy shorthand, elliptical brain-movies of her life and times, and most recently, as in her outstanding performance piece, "Fast Speaking Woman" (the title poem of her previous collection), repetitive, chant-like "songs," which bring to mind tribal shaman ceremonies. These latter, which can work hypnotically on an audience but tend to lose some of their magic on the page, point to a whole new emphasis in today's poetry – from John Giorno's reiterative "ragas" to Allen Ginsberg's "Blake-Songs" – which places the poet once again in the oral tradition, making his or her fullest statement in vocal performance – an emphasis which at least in part, I think, can be credited to the influence of such latter-day "electric" troubadours as Bob Dylan, Leonard Cohen, Rod McKuen, and others, who have reached an enormous audience by combining words and music.

The question is the familiar one of whether or not a Bob Dylan lyric sheet, for instance, amounts to a real poem, and/or whether one of Anne Waldman's poems in this mode can be judged accurately by reading it on the page. For me at least, the answer remains both yes and no. In Waldman's case, there is no mistaking the energy and high spirits of her work as printed, but for the most part the page is a poor substitute for the poet in performance. Only in the shorter poems, where the words are not dependent on a gathering rhythmic impulse that in effect must be "voiced," do you feel the experience is complete on the page, and these tend to be among the less substantial of her works, though sometimes among her most charming.

The prose selections included in *Journals & Dreams* are also among the most successful pieces, especially "Amanda" and "Letter to Joe Brainard," in which she writes of her travels in South America. At a certain hotel she was called "Lolita" by a lot of Colombian businessmen. "I decided to take it as a compliment," she writes Brainard, "but for how long?"

The poems in general tend to read quickly, and there is curiously little emotional content. As she writes in the opening long poem, "From a Continuing Work in Spanish" – "a book without a theme with many events with no person no personality." This emphasis seems to me to be a holdover from the '60s, during which many of us who then came of age tended to be beguiled by the drug-induced dissolution of any seemingly too specific, personal identity. Our minds were televisions, McLuhan told us – we being the first generation of TV babies – and, having been given drugs as a sort of high school graduation present, we were introduced to our various chemical "channels": marijuana, LSD, speed, etc.

But the '70s, I think, are clearly pointing us back to ourselves – limited as we may be, it seems increasingly clear that we are all we really have. In this respect, *Journals & Dreams* indicates to me that Anne Waldman may be at a sort of crossroads – she may remain simply a "fast speaking woman," but I wonder how much longer she can go on before this posture of "no person no personality" simply exhausts itself. She has made a genuine contribution to poetry today; perhaps now is the time for her to give more thought to her resources and direction.

New York Times Book Review

GOLDEN GATE

Golden Gate: Interviews with 5 San Francisco Poets. Edited by David Meltzer. Wingbow Press: Berkeley, California. 256 pp.

Archetype West: The Pacific Coast as a Literary Region. By William Everson. Oyez: Berkeley, California. 181 pp.

THESE TWO BOOKS explore the unique regional character of the West Coast as it reveals itself in five of its best known poets and their poetry. David Meltzer, himself a West Coast poet since the heyday of the San Francisco poetry renaissance of the middle and late '50s, has made his series of five interviews – conducted in 1969 with the poets Kenneth Rexroth, William Everson, Lawrence Ferlinghetti, Lew Welch, and Michael McClure – a kind of chronicle by generation, spanning by way of personal histories the period from the 1920s almost up to the present day.

Golden Gate was first issued in 1971 as a Ballantine paperback original and has now been reissued by Wingbow Press, the publishing arm of Book People, the small-press distributors based in Berkeley. Kenneth Rexroth, long the elder statesman of the West Coast poetry scene, speaks first:

> Large numbers of people have gone to the Northwest and California to get away from the extreme pressures of a commercial civilization. On the West Coast it is possible to beat the system . . . I would have been an utterly different human being if I had gone back to New York.

Rexroth, a man of seemingly endless erudition, is unique in his vision of the impact of political reality on American social and literary life.

The Vietnam War was a disaster because, he tells us, until it "got hot, the dominant tendency in the movement in America was anarchist-pacifist . . . and religious in various ways." By placing American radicals "in the ridiculous position of supporting the foreign policies of Ho Chi Minh, or Chairman Mao, or Fidel Castro, or Tito, or Israel," the war gave "a political complexion to the movement which it had almost got rid of."

Or consider his explanation of the cliquish character of the literary establishment during the '50s: "Since most of the people, except the Southern agrarians, had been one-time Stalinists, they just took over all the techniques of Stalinism . . . you know, hatchet reviews and logrolling and wire-pulling and controls of foundations and academic jobs and so forth. . . ."

William Everson, interviewed just after he left the Order of Dominican Monks in which he was known as Brother Antoninus – he left in order to marry – speaks with a palpable sense of the urgency of this transition for him:

> I find there are two different worlds, the domestic world and the monastic world. . . . But it seems to me that once the domestic life . . . is constituted as a permeable reflective form, then the prophetic role, the poet's role, may draw on it with the same accessibility as it does on the monastic life. What I'm saying is that, monasticism or domesticity, the prophetic function must go on.

Lawrence Ferlinghetti speaks of his concern about the proliferation of government money in sponsorship of small-press publications, in which he feels an implicit compromise of the integrity of the recipient; and "then too [he is speaking, remember, as the Vietnam War continued on] someone in another country – a radical in France or Germany – reads about your taking this money, and they don't see the rationalization and the various gradations of your reasoning. All they see is the fact that you took U.S. government money. . . ."

Later he comments on the situation of the public poet: "Not only do you have to have poems that have a good deal of 'public surface' and might be considered performance poems, but it takes a very exceptional voice to make it with an enormous audience. Allen Ginsberg is one of the few who makes it. He can be on the same program with a rock group because he has such a marvelously full voice."

Lew Welch, the poet who disappeared with his gun into the foothills of the Sierra Nevada in 1971 and who spent some time working as a San Francisco cab driver, emphasizes in contrast the one-to-one relationship of the poet with his nonpoet peers:

> Now you find you have to say to your cab-driving, pool-playing buddies that you are a poet sooner or later. You have to tell them, you have to let them in on it, you have to. Otherwise you are cheating them of your friendship. And when you do, you get this: "Mm-mm, uh-uh, oh, yeah. . ."
>
> Anyway, I told them at this pool game. I said, "By the way, do you know that I am a poet? If you don't mind, I would like to read you one." And I read them "After Anacreon" [Welch's poem about driving a cab]. And they stopped chalking their cues, and they stopped playing, and they really started listening. And when I finished, they said, "Goddamn, Lewie, I don't know whether or not that is a poem, but that is the way it *is* to drive a cab."
>
> I said, "Thanks, I am just testing it."

Michael McClure, the last and youngest poet interviewed in the book, anticipates an emphasis of the '70s in a discussion of meditation versus television:

> There are several kinds of meditation. Let me give you two. One is the kind that is done in Subud. You move your arms and legs randomly in a darkened room with your eyes closed. You shout or sing or chant rhythmically at the same time. Try to think while you are doing that! It's impossible. Your screen is blank. Totally blank. And your screen being totally blank, you are getting a feedback of your own sensations. . . . You realize you are the universe. Afterwards you feel high. You really feel good. An hour of that is fantastically rewarding!
>
> The other kind of meditation is much more complex. You

do it through a series of studies and rejections and accept-
ances. You learn to empty the reticular system of your neu-
ronal screen. Either one works. What I am saying is that TV
is not emptying your screen, it is only filling it up enough to
white it out. You're not getting any feedback. When it gets
blank you get feedback. After watching TV, notice that you feel
exhausted. After meditation, either Subud-type meditation
or Hindu Buddhist-type meditation, you feel invigorated.

Archetype West: The Pacific Coast As a Literary Region seems to have
been one of William Everson's first projects after leaving the Dominican order, and it sets for itself the task of chronologically tracing the
inception, development, apotheosis, and current embodiment of
what he calls the Western archetype as it's revealed in the literature
of the West. Responding initially to a request from the magazine
American Libraries for an essay on the literary character of the West
as a particular region of the United States, Everson approached his
subject from "this archetypal point of view because I am not able to
make sense of regionalism from any other perspective," and he
ended up with a full-length book.

What exactly is the Western archetype? Everson identifies its
apotheosis as the work of the poet Robinson Jeffers, by way of exposition quoting from a speech delivered by the young Santayana in
1911 to the Philosophical Union in Berkeley. Santayana assailed the
prevailing genteel tradition as a kind of "enervated transcendental-
ism" in which Americans "thought themselves in the throes of some
rapturous interpenetration of mind and nature – when they were
doing little else than taking the air." In California, Santayana saw
the possibility of a relationship between the "virgin and prodigious
world" and individual humans that would be so direct and powerful that it would give the lie to the systems which the "European
Genteel Tradition has handed down since Socrates" – systems Santayana characterized as "inspired by the conceited notion that man,
or human reason, or the human distinction between good and evil,
is the center and pivot of the universe." The speech anticipated the
philosophy of "inhumanism" later advocated by Jeffers, who was
twenty-four and living in Los Angeles at the time.

Almost from its inception, this archetype has provided a resource for the now-burgeoning ecology movement, which seeks the ideal that all forms of life be given the same respect that the human race has reserved exclusively for itself. The realization that we ourselves are only another link in what the poet Gary Snyder (whose work Everson sees as the archetype's clearest present embodiment) describes as "that ecstatic Mutual Offering called the Food Chain" involves a profound restructuring of our understanding, somewhat equivalent, perhaps, to the realization that the earth was not the center of the universe.

Everson brings a meditative mind to this material, and I found his book extraordinary in its continuous receptivity. He has a chapter on John Steinbeck that seems to me to be especially illuminating, and one on Ken Kesey that includes the following paragraph, in which he questions Charles Reich's assertion in *The Greening of America* that one of Kesey's novels "comes closest to being in the fullest sense a work of the new consciousness." He describes the hero:

A racist, a sexist, an anticommunitarian, a scoffing agnostic, he yet affirms the individual's need to stand upon his own intrinsic resources, eschewing any recourse other than to himself, whether it be race, community, patriotism, love, or religion. This, in fact, is his primal power, the impulse that grabs the gut. But there is nothing new about it. By it the mighty sequoias fell, the buffalo vanished, the cities were spawned, the high rivers polluted. If this is the new consciousness it can only be circa 1849.

Village Voice

ECHO CHAMBERS

The Collected Poems: 1956–1974. By Edward Dorn. Four Seasons Foundation: Bolinas, California. 277 pp.

EDWARD DORN belongs to that unique generation of American poets who came of age between the Beat Generation of the middle and late '50s and the rock culture led by the Beatles, the Rolling Stones, and Bob Dylan half a decade later. Among his contemporaries, he is perhaps closest in temper and outlook to LeRoi Jones, with whom he shared a rare friendship (Jones's book *The Dead Lecturer* is dedicated to Dorn) before the fall of 1965, when Jones repudiated his life in the predominantly white culture of New York's Lower East Side, and split to Newark to embrace the black community, and with it his own black heritage, ultimately changing his name to Imamu Amiri Baraka.

Dorn, being white, might have envied Jones so decisive an option. While the poets shared an essentially lyric gift, each felt increasingly compelled to make his poetry an instrument of social consciousness. Jones was able to explicitly resolve this tension by assuming the position of a black militant, and henceforth writing exclusively for the black community, while Dorn moved to England for several years and wrote with an increasingly theoretical emphasis.

Then, in the late '60s, perhaps in some measure liberated by the burgeoning rock culture, he wrote the *Gunslinger* books, a dramatic narrative in which voices of enormous variety in tone and outlook are constantly shifting through the lines. It seems to me one of the two or three outstanding achievements of American poetry during the '60s – a kind of "exploded" narrative in which the voice fragments are like modes of consciousness recurring throughout the whole in an effect like an echo chamber: perhaps the poet's mind itself in the psychedelic explosion of his time.

The Collected Poems: 1956–1974, which excludes the *Gunslinger* books ("evoked," Dorn writes in his preface, "on another scale"), is an otherwise complete eighteen-year retrospective of Dorn's poetry. Here he is at the beginning, with unabashed lyricism and his beautifully individual ear:

VAQUERO

The cowboy stands beneath
a brick-orange moon. The top
of his oblong head is blue, the sheath
of his hips
is too.

In the dark brown night
your delicate cowboy stands quite still.
His plain hands are crossed.
His wrists are embossed white.

In the background night is a house,
has a blue chimney top,
Yi Yi, the cowboy's eyes
are blue. The top of the sky
is too.

And here, too, is the middle Dorn, the ending of a poem dedicated to Jones and his wife, Hetti, "Idaho Out":

... Idaho
is cut
by an elbow
of mountain that swings
down, thus she is
cut off by geologies she says
I'm sure

are natural
but it is truly the West
as no other place,
ruined by an ambition and religion
cut, by a cowboy use of her nearly virgin self

     unannealed
by a real placement
                this,
this
is the birthplace
of Mr. Pound
and Hemingway in his own mouth
chose to put a shotgun.

This tone is carried through the poems written during his years in England, which are, for the most part, long social meditations, in which Dorn yet sustains his music:

. . . My mother, moving slowly in a grim kitchen
and my stepfather moving slowly down the green rows of corn
these are my unruined and damned hieroglyphs.
     Because they form
the message of men stooping down
in my native land, and father an entire conglomerate
of need and wasted vision. All the children
were taught the pledge of Allegiance, and the land was pledged
to private use, the walnut dropped in the autumn on
          the ground
green, and lay black in the dead grass in the spring.

Finally, in the more recent poems, especially the cycle of "Love Songs," there is a return to the lyricism of the opening poems, but of a quieter, more tender order, as in "song 2":

Inside the late nights of last week
under the cover of ourselves

you went to sleep in my arms
and last night too
you were in some alarm
of your dream
       some tableau
an assembling of signs
from your troubled day glows
and trembles, your limbs
divine with sleep
gather and extend their flesh
along mine
and this I surround, all this
I had my arms around

It can be hoped that the '70s will see America further into a time
when its poets will find less in it to regret, when poets like Edward
Dorn and LeRoi Jones will no longer be separated from friendship.

Village Voice

A BREATH

Jaguar Skies. Poems by Michael McClure. New Directions: New York. 100 pp.

MICHAEL MCCLURE'S POETRY is unique. He is an unabashed visionary and takes all the risks of that stance to make his statement. His poetry seldom indulges in, for instance, humor; almost all of his poems are "lived" moments of heightened insight, and over the course of a whole book one can grow homesick for the mundane. Perhaps most crucially, McClure has chosen to structure his poems by centering each line rather than using the standard left margin, which makes of the reader's eye a sort of pioneer in the uncharted territory of each poem. There is nothing to fall back on here – nothing but the poet's energy and poise in his explorations.

Having said that, I should add that McClure's poetry seems to me among the best, among the most beautiful and joyous, being written these days. He has created his own form and idiom and gone on to become an absolute master of it. His new book, *Jaguar Skies*, which is mostly made up of shorter works, seems to me one of his most successful. There is a new unity of tone here, a quieter and more relaxed seeing without any diminution of vision. Here is "A Breath":

HOW
SWEET
TO
BE
A
ROSE
BY

CANDLE
LIGHT
or
a
worm
by
full
moon.
See the hop-
ping flight
a cricket makes.
Nature loves
the absence of
mistakes.

McClure was among the first poets of the counterculture to recon-
sider the drug orientation of the 1960s, and having been one of the
first to explore the psychedelics, he is now making a strong statement for a return from drugs' "temporary alchemy" (as he put it in
"99 Theses" from his previous collection, *September Blackberries*).
The central theme of *Jaguar Skies* is ecology – a perfect theme for
McClure's consistently "biological" emphasis. He sees all matter as
a unity of atoms and molecules, his own human "meat" a "cousin"
to "eagles and deer." This is how "To a Golden Lion Marmoset – an
endangered primate species" begins:

OH BEAUTIFUL LITTLE FACE,
PEERING THROUGH
THE DAWN
OF TIME,
THE GOLDEN FUR UPON YOUR
CHEEKS
is precious as a rhyme.

Indeed, he sees poetry itself as "a muscular principle – an athletic
song or whisper of fleshly thought," and in his poems he is able to
make the vision come alive. His lines seem to hold the mysteries of

spirit and flesh, time and space, in a way similar to the way a person or an animal, a mountain or a flower, hold them. To read his work, then, is to view the beauty as well as the riddle. If he pays a certain price for his vision, he does so in order to give us not a small gift. As in the ending of "At Night on the River," he lets us *see*:

Let
us
prepare
to love this place
before we leave it.
Let our skulls sprout
invisible tentacles
of sympathy
for birth
and death
for we are but
a breath
of fairy substance
falling on the endless
– tufts of fluff
upon the Amazon.

Village Voice

REEDIES

Selected Poems. By Lew Welch. Preface by Gary Snyder. Edited by Donald Allen. Grey Fox Press: Bolinas, California. 94 pp.

The Kindness of Strangers. By Philip Whalen. Grey Fox Press: Bolinas, California. 57 pp.

IN THE LATE 1940s, Lew Welch, Gary Snyder, and Philip Whalen were classmates at Reed College. Although all three have been identified with the San Francisco Poetry Renaissance of the mid-50s – in which the Beat Generation surfaced as a social and literary phenomenon – they are all, it seems to me, quite different from the Beats, and in my mind at least they constitute a kind of movement unto themselves. All, for instance, tend to be less flashy writers than the Beats, quieter, more involved with nature and less media oriented, and all share an absolute dedication to the craft and spirit of poetry that has made them central to any assessment of the work of their generation.

Lew Welch is a strange case. Marianne Moore singled him out in her review of Donald Allen's definitive anthology, *The New American Poetry 1945–1960*, on the front page of the old *New York Herald Tribune Book Review*, but Welch was somehow never able to get a good-sized collection of his poetry printed, while most of his peers, if not exactly prosperous, at least had a book or two to their credit. Then, in May of 1971, while living in his van on Gary Snyder's land in the foothills of the Sierra Nevada, he disappeared with his gun, leaving a note appointing Donald Allen his literary executor. His body was never found.

Selected Poems represents Donald Allen's condensation, or per-

haps a better word would be concentration, of his initial collection
of Welch's poems, *Ring of Bone: Collected Poems, 1950–1971.* This
new book, about a third the length of the first volume, is the essen-
tial Welch: combining a personable playfulness with unremitting
attention to each word, one line at a time. There is the design of a
whole lifetime within this brief volume, and it is a clear registration
of the poet at odds with his society. The ending of one of his first
works, "Chicago Poem," focuses Welch's life's drama in the instance
of that city:

> You can't fix it. You can't make it go away.
>   I don't know what you're going to do about it,
> But I know what I'm going to do about it. I'm just
>   going to walk away from it. Maybe
> A small part of it will die if I'm not around
>
>   feeding it anymore.

Welch, who struggled with alcoholism, seemingly spent his life
alternating mountain hermitages with urban life, writing about
each with the humanity that is perhaps his primary hallmark. He
doesn't separate himself from his environment, whatever its nature,
by any sense of superiority, but rather he perceives its dynamics by
giving himself without restraint to its reality. After visiting the top
of the Empire State Building, for instance, and then taking the ele-
vator down, Welch encounters Manhattan:

> In the lobby are people who are really doing it, not like us,
> just looking around. They wear the current costume
>   and read
> the office directories beside the banks and banks of
> elevators. I realize there are offices in the Empire State
> Building! It is not just a tower to look from!
>
> It all starts coming in, on the street. Each one is going
> somewhere, thinking. Many are moving their lips, talking

to themselves. In 2 blocks I am walking as fast as they
are. We all agree to wait when the light turns red.

In this sense, the poems point to a kind of morality rooted in the
senses, in receiving the impulses of each environment and finding
out exactly where they lead. In a poem written in a mountain her-
mitage, Welch recounts his experience of seeing himself in a clear
stream:

> and vowed,
> always to be open to it
> that all of it
> might flow through

Philip Whalen's new collection of poems has been issued simultaneously with Lew Welch's book by Donald Allen, and it is dedicated
to Welch. Whalen, who for the past several years has been an or-
dained Zen priest in residence at San Francisco's Zen Center, is perhaps the most natural writer of his generation, in the sense that his
writing embodies a kind of happy exercise of all his faculties. He
seems less to be transcribing his experience than writing it into being,
sometimes creating a magical reality. This is "The Vision of Delight":

> The man driving the expensive car
> May have no relation to the woman sitting beside him
> Neither of them might be related to the small girl
> Who sat in the center of the back seat, leaning immobile
> Against the back rest.
> Her dress was white her hair all neatly arranged
> Grotesque white fangs protruded from her mouth
> Without distorting it.
> She looked serenely straight ahead.
> She was the queen attended by the court lady and chauffeur
> Not going to the Safeway store, clearly not needing
> The automobile, who can appear anywhere any time
> Such is her tremendous power

In addition to several collections of poetry, Whalen has published two highly enjoyable novels, *You Didn't Even Try* and *Imaginary Speeches for a Brazen Head*, in which his prose is as accomplished as his poetry. It's a mystery to me why these books are not more celebrated, except that they are about men and women simply living in the world, enjoying it and not enjoying it, without doing anything overly dramatic. What makes the books fun to read are their characters and Whalen's prose. Very revolutionary.

The Kindness of Strangers is the latest installment of Whalen's poetic monologue, a kind of interior decoration of the spirit. One finds oneself lighting up inside after a few pages, simply because the surroundings are so down-to-earth luxurious. Here, for instance, is the short opening poem, "Eamd," which sets the tone for what follows:

> How well I know, how clearly I see
> The ideal he aims for, the quality
>   he creates:
> A cloudy green forest, a gentle wood
>   full of *rishi* and musicians. . .
>
>   "the solemn elephant reposing in the
>   shade. . ."

Philip Whalen and Lew Welch have yet to be celebrated as they deserve to be. Gary Snyder, another fine poet, has fared the best of the Reed triumvirate, winning the 1975 Pulitzer Prize for his collection *Turtle Island*.

American Book Review

APPENDIX: BEGINNINGS
1964–1969

CREELEY'S NOVEL

ROBERT CREELEY does a simple but rare thing. In each form he uses – up to now poetry, criticism, and a huge amount of letter writing – he insists on being "personal." That is, he allows his own mind to dominate, to dictate, formal procedure. He is the man who said it: "Form is only an extension of content"; and in his own work it is *consciously* so. He is, for instance, the only writer I know in whom I cannot find one rhetorical instance, i.e., "fitting" a sound: Creeley insists the opposite. And the forms themselves are of course changed by this, in the sense that they are "re-formed" each time to his personal measures. Also as a consequence, Creeley may maintain a consistency this way as "person" that is "trans-formal." He is one of the minority of poets who write good prose and is even rarer for writing prose that is "like" his poetry. And finally, when he takes up a new form, as he has just now the novel, he is not bothered by the usual problems. There is no question of "what" to write about, that is, what "will go"; he has said that his distinctions between the forms are purely technical, simply how to make the new form suit his purpose for it – fit. The rewards of this way of writing are exceptional. Creeley has a record that seems to me perfect: he is – by method! – "master" of any form. Witness: *The Island.**

John is a young writer living with his wife and children on an island that sounds like Majorca, where Creeley once lived. He is distracted and/or dissatisfied with his work, and in his pause from it come long, wonderfully elaborate reflections. John is a Creeley-like, endlessly self-analyzing intelligence. (It seems rare that someone actually thinks in novels.) His trouble only seems a lack of some

---

* *The Island.* A novel by Robert Creeley. Scribner: New York. 190 pp.

sure referent to test himself on. He craves company. Completely at odds with his wife, John keeps – terribly – "missing" her. In the last scene, a brilliant climax, in the middle of the night, after a fight, he hysterically supposes her suicide, chasing the whole beach for her, only to come back and find her. "I thought you were dead," he says, "but I was wrong." So the book ends.

A history is I think the best description. The kind that is I think especially common to people who get with language on anything like primary terms. That is, the words can so easily take over here, come unpinned to any instance, become instances themselves instead. As the words with John, on and on – where they stop, god knows. Like the suicide. Where did it come from? Creeley, it seems to me, is obsessed with this danger, of words coming and going on their own.

And all this bears relation to the whole body of Creeley's work. He is one writer who will not be "possessed," that is, let go (let's say like Kerouac) to "what comes." He honors and holds the words absolutely to what Cid Corman called his "single-mind." He refers the words *back* on it, tests them according to it. As John is words, Creeley "uses" them.

Apropos, *The Island*, as a title, seems a kind of multiple pun – at once John himself; the literal island – the place; and finally perhaps island as an enclave of unity, correspondence, and commonness between things – which is where John would get to, but is hopeless, as Creeley demonstrates, until the words are secured back from all flights, however interesting, and put in their place.

Creeley has written an excellent novel. And one that is all his own, an original, very much of a "single" mind. For these very qualities it is also a characteristic work, one more piece of the growing whole.

SENTENCES

A FRIEND OF MINE – he is dead now – arrived years ago and went directly into a book, refused to get into conversation with me. Well, it is a year ago nearly.

First though, he *did* take off his shoes, filling the room.

He was one of the people I had much trouble reacting to, and I still do. In his letters (I later found out) are many lies about his life. He had a very clear voice and a peremptory manner, but he was somehow without authority. Perhaps it was my age, being two years older than he was, and, as he seemed very much a younger version of me, thinking myself – *feeling* – wiser.

When I was told he died, I was shocked. I couldn't feel anything. I hadn't cried in a very long time and didn't then.

I *did* have a dream later that I cried after. But it would be presumptuous to equate that dream with any final realization of his death. It had nothing to do with it.

It remains for me like a huge headline in which I feel – only the ink.

Or listening to a voice and not hearing what is being said.

SENTENCES II

THE SHOES DIDN'T FIT, but my idea was that they hadn't been broken in. I spent the whole summer in them. At night I would lie back under the window and feel the little air, the sheet, my hair against the small pillow, whatever, in that time, which to get through was my leaving and returning there, the room as I felt it, my hair as I would feel it, in there.

And so private, as that was, waking in my arms, and putting the shirt, pants, socks on; and the weather, just so heavy, or hot; the privacy of seeing or not; and the shoes – or boots really – which made me limp slightly. At the job, no one noticed; in the street, anyone might guess it was my legs, or perhaps even the shoes. I was seeing no one at all, if that would have made a difference.

If I had known it was the shoes – boots – I would have gotten another pair.

I did buy sneakers, but my feet were swollen, and the arch was just as painful if not worse wearing them. I couldn't get them to work if they *were* the right size, which they were, until my feet unswelled. And they also got hot through the day, so they were worse than the boots.

Probably one weekend I stayed as much as I could out of either pair, but that wasn't long enough.

And it is the boots. Exactly. Though just too for me to recognize, for me to do anything about, that tight, for me to do anything but put them on and take them off, almost counting the days, but not on doing that. When I got out, which I did, of the job, and the apartment, and then bought a new pair, etc., then it would – the story – would work out that way, finally *is* the boots. But it wouldn't, isn't, until then.

SENTENCES III

THERE'S NOTHING in this box. To look backwards as coming forward; or days stopped. I miss them in Italian churches. There were houses pushing into the hush, perfectly suited memory. "Dam you," indications of hives, pen once again turning in this light. One of us laughed, maybe both. But she remembered thread to inflict the golden dark path of breath; and the chance to disappear.

We responded with "Now it is over and Hands point to a dim, a vivid machine," glory having no slow design. Though we were soon discussing his broken sandwich: "You're not very brave, you press the point." I forget how it, the fact, for example, talking Pat, started to help me out.

Others wept across the lake. That it hurt like hell, odd love, economy, then the hammer, dazzling bold strokes – I AIN'T GONNA . . . I had the courage. She opened but she remembered and checked herself. "Flourish and bear any time at all."

Behind the magical Tom-machine: the cinema, decrying sin; irrelevant in the garden of my American citizen. Poetry about heterosexual contacts, the bodies of my suffering, mark my ways (a mulatto girl) end in taverns. The practical aspects, a ribbon of witty dialogue across the fact. Up and around.

She painted with fruit, developed a machine, celluloid, under the eyes of these states. First A talks, then B. Her neuroses. The car door aglitter with green, some lie rotting. "Kick me out," she breathed.

"In the dark night I would like a silk cover."

Today, May 6th, 1965, on the corner of Madison
Avenue and 59th St. a shock ran through my
body and I found myself flying – at 68th St. and
Madison I came down and walked the half block
to The Right Bank where I had originally planned
to go for coffee. I haven't seen a newspaper or a
news broadcast since so I don't know if I was
noticed. It was astonishing and delightful.

FINLAY'S PRESENT

I DON'T KNOW very much about "Concretist" poetry, of which Ian Hamilton Finlay is the outstanding practitioner, about its origin and development, that is. My guess is that the word relates to children's chalk art, the way words and drawing are combined there, the heart with the names in it, etc., the shape and sense as integral. . .

In any case, this is a little different – here it's finding a shape and sense in the words alone. Visual poems. Some words "seen" together.

And one feels particularly in Finlay's work, that he discovered his forms on the page – literally seeing the words.

He might begin with a single word, or letter even. That is a very fluid, multiple possibility. For example, how an object changes in different contexts. How a word changes with one letter dropped, or added to it, or not even added, but placed in proximity.

These works are full of that mystery. Some of them are hard to "understand." Edward Dahlberg wrote: "Present is an absolute sphinx." These works are acts within and of it. They change as they are read, or perhaps better, *seen*.

Finlay is also, probably very relevantly, a printer. He is the publisher of the Wild Hawthorn Press. In this book,* which he published, the poems are done in red ink on good, very white, stock. It isn't anything to be carried around for a day. It's 75¢. The minute I got it I wanted to get home, wash my hands, and find out what was going on.

---

* *Telegrams from My Windmill*. Poems by Ian Hamilton Finlay. Wild Hawthorn Press.

A NOTE ON GIACOMETTI

THE SCULPTURE

GIACOMETTI'S SCULPTURE is unique. It makes a special light that remains constant wherever it is viewed. The sculpted object is the result of this light. The sculpture and its light are the same event, no matter the actual light of the viewing.

As its craterous, "invaded" surface embodies it, the light of a Giacometti is fantastically powerful. It is so strong it tends to encroach, even to deform, the physical matter it exposes. The figures are "lit" with it, so skinny because the light has blasted out their bulk.

Still the light is apparently harmless – the objects that embody it, even at its most predatory, seem oblivious to it. There is that sculpture of the dog, ravaged by it, as if about to disappear in it, and still just a dog, in the swing of his trot.

THE PAINTINGS

Almost monochromatic, riddled with hundreds of lines of slightly varying shades, these paintings hold so powerful a light that it works in an animate distraction or counterpoint to the literal subject matter. One can barely realize an image before the lines begin to flash independently of it and the painting turns into a light. The descriptive subject of the painting is always on the verge of obliteration in the actual instance of light the painting is. The numberless lines seem to split literal space so that it is no longer objective – suddenly a pure, vibrating light.

Walking I am reading in the *New York Review of Books*. How much of Marcel is Proust? or, how much of Proust is Marcel? Out of this riddle we have derived the current vogue of "psycho-derived the current vogue of "psycho-portraits" of authors as one of their own characters. It's Election Day, 6 o'clock so the polls have now opened.

NOTES ON AMERICAN PROSE [1965]

WILLIAM BURROUGHS

WILLIAM BURROUGHS has expanded his three-column news-paper format to include photographs. Examples – excerpts from a new book for Grove – appeared in *Lines 5* and *6*. When I visited him early last summer at his loft on Center Street, he was just finishing some pages in this new mode based on the last words of Dutch Schultz, the prose columns worked around photographs of the St. Valentine's Day corpses. He said the whole story for Schultz hinges on the number twenty-two. It was the twenty-second, one of Schultz's bodyguards was shot on 22nd Street a few hours earlier, he was twenty-two, etc. We also discussed concrete and/or visual poetry which Burroughs is very interested in now, though he was not in touch with – and in fact knew very little of – Finlay, Furnival, Houedard, et al.

Burrough's *Nova Express* seems to me to have forecast his grow-ing visual interest. There are so many dashes on each page of that book that the prose itself has an immediate spatial reality; the images flash one on another – many impossible to grasp – as if in a dream and/or traveling by at great speed. And one is *reading* faster and faster; it's "about" an interplanetary war. The first time I tried read-ing it, though, after twenty pages I couldn't go on. The speed of it didn't seem right. I was trying to read it slowly, and those dashes were getting terrible: before a phrase could come clear there would be another one. I put the book down and figured it for a graph of some acute form of spatial distraction – a man turning here and there and here and there so fast he doesn't know what he's seeing. The book isn't that. It's a real story, and there's a surprisingly healthful presence to it – I felt great reading it the second time – but I had to go just as fast as my eyes took me, trust Burroughs that it would be fine.

FIELDING DAWSON

The second-fastest writing in the world is by Fielding Dawson, and in his *Thread* he really lets go. But then he comes back, it works out, makes a "form," etc. It does, but a little too neatly, it seemed to me. As if he were out flying a kite, say, and it had suddenly gone too far out, literally gone out of sight, and then he realized it was dark, too, and he had to pull it in, finish, and he couldn't see the kite again until it was almost on top of him. And/or there he is – in the middle of it – the kite, even the spool maybe, gotten away from him and racing through the grass, and it's dark, and he runs after it and bumps into a tree and shouts thank god! a tree! and sure enough (he's right) the spool's somehow caught on the tree, and he winds up and it's all over. It gets very way-out and then it gets very simple, not to say simplistic. I wonder if Dawson wouldn't have done better not to have let it go so far out, to have kept it all closer in. His description of a man and his dog at a party is the best writing of the book for me, and it's on the first page.

LEROI JONES

LeRoi Jones's *The System of Dante's Hell* slowly metamorphoses out of impressionistic prose/poetry into first-rate narrative. The transformation is both formally and substantively chronological; that is, it begins almost incomprehensibly and then gradually gets clearer, working from childhood through and out of adolescence. I liked the book very much; it's not at all just the collection I suspected it would be, having read many of its parts published separately earlier.

TOM VEITCH

Tom Veitch's *Literary Days* is a wild prose pastiche including direct cops from Rilke, Henry Miller, Burroughs, and I'm sure lots of others I didn't recognize. The book was put together by Ted Berrigan (Veitch says it's not really his book – !) from two book-length manuscripts. It's very funny, but the first time I read it, I read it entirely straight and thought it was very "interesting." Veitch is Burroughs's favorite new writer, and that's as close as I'll get to describing his work. He's written a number of very good short stories, so he's better than a great collagist. He could be a genius. He's just now joined a monastery though and apparently destroyed his new works. But he's only twenty-five and chances are he'll be publishing soon again.

TED BERRIGAN

Ted Berrigan's novel-in-progress, *Looking for Chris* – excerpts from which have appeared or are about to appear in *C*, *Mother*, and *Art and Literature* – is serious. The sections I've seen are short-paragraphed, interesting, boring, interesting boring, mostly incomprehensible, and *not* funny. And he keeps on writing.

ROSS MACDONALD

Ross Macdonald, the mystery writer, is very good. His *The Chill* is especially excellent, and so is his latest, *Black Money.* . . Mystery novels seem a very rich possibility right now: a way of getting down all the extremity amidst all the compromise. Chandler and Hammet and Macdonald render a whole cosmos in their details. It always amazes me, for example, when the detective has to lie to the police. And where the detective stops, where he can't go on even if it's "right" to, and still be in business. Nothing ever gets quite cleaned up. Everybody does as well as possible. As against the neatness, the completeness, of the murders. I wonder what Norbert Wiener would have said about that.

JOE PINELLI

Joe Pinelli has so far written two books – called *Book I* and *Book II* – each of which contains wonderful prose. He's published so far only in *Lines 6*, selections I chose from *Book I*. His favorite writer is Henry Miller, but his own work is nothing like Miller's. It reminds me, surprisingly, of Fellini's *8½* and *Juliet of the Spirits*, the way he gets a wild fantasy to *happen*. His greatest enthusiasm right now is the New Music, of Cecil Taylor, Archie Shepp, Albert Ayler, and his friends Frank Smith and Burton Greene, and he's writing a lot for the jazz reviews as well as working on a new book. He's twenty-seven or twenty-eight and has a beard and talks softly, but he puts down the whole literary scene these days for not having enough *"feeling!"* The only poet who's made any impression on him is McClure, but he doesn't like his political tack. He just moved into New York City. "I'm ready to dig it," he said.

JOHN CHEEVER

John Cheever – yes, the old man – is a great prose writer. His latest collection of short stories, *The Brigadier and the Golf Widow*, contains some of the most exciting works I've read. He publishes mostly in *The New Yorker*, he's won the National Book Award, and he's probably richer than everybody, but he's absolutely first-rate.

He presents a very unlikely suburbia, a very unlikely commuter; he does not report minutiæ, as O'Hara, Marquand, etc. Instead his people are related in a continuum of struggle and play of real grandeur – a continuum alternately relieved and heightened in their consciousness of the physical loveliness around them.

And Cheever knows how to go all out – he can pull off the wildest scenes. His taste is immaculate. There's a Kafka and an O'Casey going at once. It's beautiful. It really is.

A LETTER TO
THE VILLAGE VOICE [1966]

DEAR SIR:

Jack Newfield's attack on the
English folk singer Donovan (*Voice*,
February 24) confuses promotion –
and the character of an audience –
with the music.

> Aram Saroyan
> West 85th Street

A POEM OF A LIFE*

From A 1 (1928):

The lights dim, and the brain when the flesh dims.

From A 5 (1930):

The trees showing sunlight
Sunlight trees,
Words ranging forms.

From A 12 (1950–1951):

The best man learns of himself
To bring rest to others.

. . .

To begin a song:
If you cannot recall,
Forget.

. . .

How fathom his will
Who had taught himself to be simple
Everything should be as simple as it can be,
Says Einstein,
But not simpler.

---

* *A 1–12*, a poem of a life, by Louis Zukofsky. Doubleday/Paris Review Editions.
* *A 13–21*, a poem of a life, by Louis Zukofsky. Doubleday/Paris Review Editions.

169

. . .

What the mind sees
And the eyes see – the
Shape of their ground, the same.

. . .

If love exists, why remember it?

. . .

Who understands
Loves and sees,
Believes what he knows
The horse has large eyes

. . .

This music
Moved by a thought to a hand –

. . .

To wolf crumbs
From a flying roll
Eat raw cabbages
Whole

. . .

The mind is not free to remember or forget
Anything the opened hand feels.

. . .

Repentance
Twice unhappy
Pitiable,
Pitiful

. . .

Red crayon redder than the red paper it is on.

From A 13 (1960):

>   The paroled
>   Forgets his prison quickly.
>
>   . . .
>
>   The universe simply does. . .
>
>   . . .
>
>   To recover
>   Your coat don't
>   Lose your shirt, don't kick down
>
>   The ladder you stepped up
>
>   . . .
>
>   Nature
>   Sorts from unbreathing things
>
>   To animals in unbroken sequence
>   Interposing life scarcely
>   Animal, jellyfish, sea-lungs
>
>   Their lives simply
>   Plants separated
>   From the ground
>
>   A tailstring
>   Nature gives it
>   To insects of fierce
>
>   Disposition –
>
>   . . .
>
>   An ox – horns of
>   Such length – he must

Walk backwards to graze.
Brain is the cause of sleep
Why drowsy persons

Hang the head.

. . .

Man should not work
At the same time
With his mind and his body.

. . .

The mix of sun and breeze

. . .

Turning the head to look at
The people back of you
And the children in front, under, around
In summer the benches filled with people.

. . .

20, 40 and 60
While the oldest knows only
That he has breathed
20 years more than the older
And 40 more than the younger. . .

From A 14 (1964):

Where are my
distance glasses, reading
lenses, focus of

the aging – I
stumbled into the
TV – 'you want?

to be on
television' – C.

. . .

The child once
cried twice first
on hearing how

he was born
and again one
wail when his

grandpa died. . .

. . .

Twain's Jim with
integration *behind* him. . .

. . .

Dim eye looks
where the lively
mind once skipped. . .

. . .

That Was The
Week That Was

. . .

your place so
clean Bill said
you could eat

off the floor
I wouldn't suggest
it, stopped him

. . .

See
land,
flowers

Drink
hot
tea!

> . . .

In not
looking for metaphor

our worlds do
fly together: if
there are not

too many words.

> . . .

an escaped cat
ran down three
flights of stairs

a little boy
after, he caught
it and climbed

back up the
three flights and
before closing the

door on it,
stroked it, 'you
pussy stay upstairs.

now *I'll* go
downstairs.'

From A 15 (1964):

>   Naked on face of white rock – sea.

>   . . .

>   I was dreaming a high hole in rock
>   from which flowed the Seine
>   because that was how it looked
>   and was showing my father
>   of whom I rarely dream back to
>   its source when the doorbell
>   rang. . .

From A 18 (1964–1966):

>   Forgetting: that's all I need say or remember.

From A 21 (1967):

>   – caterpillars
>   moving not unlike
>   waves of the
>   sea.

>   . . .

>   . . . not being able
>   to leave undone what
>   is doing

AFTERWORD:
SHIFTING LIGHT

MY MIND TENDS to slip away at the word "infinity." The mind, after all, is good at establishing definitions, making discriminations, identifying borderlines and boundaries, and infinity doesn't allow for that. It just keeps going.

Nonetheless, one has a sort of cultural patrimony that includes bits and pieces of Einstein's theory of relativity, and occasionally I'll fix on the statement, for instance, that when a body achieves the speed of light, it becomes infinite. The speed of light, 186,000 miles per second, Einstein tells us, is interchangeable with infinity.

Paradoxically, if infinity is without limit, light, its counterpart, can be characterized only in the specific terms of what its presence allows us to see. My notorious one-word poem, written in 1965 –

lighght

– is a construction that adds an element to the word "light" as if to render light itself more palpable, as if the word holds the phenomenon.

Recently it occurred to me that the problem I had thinking about infinity was that I was trying to envision it quantitatively. If light, or the speed of light, is interchangeable with infinity, perhaps that means that the change from a very great distance to infinity is qualitative rather than quantitative.

Is it possible that infinity is the phenomenon of light itself?

Light exists in its embrace of what is outside itself: paradoxically self-dispossession is its very being.

177

Likewise, letting go of the specific baggage one brings to the table and taking cognizance of what is across the table, out there, we light on something, the saying goes, as if we ourselves in that moment imitate the action of light in taking cognizance of something outside the self.

AT A BUS STOP

I turned to
an accumulation of women

the instant
a break

the light was so clear
the forms

that instant
exceeded names

outsped
the words

which
follow

follow slowly
like thunder

its lights

This early poem of mine depicts an incident in which the self is lost for a moment in the play of light. What is seen is both very vivid and not easily identifiable ("exceeded names"). Like light, the self for a moment becomes indistinguishable from what it encounters. In my experience, this moment is both extraordinary and full of reassurance, despite the fact that one's identity seems to slip its moorings.

What happens here, I hypothesize, is that in duplicating the action of light, the self for an instant joins the infinite play of the universe.

The reassurance – a kind of cosmic corroboration felt in one's depths – seems to happen in one's transformation in the moment from noun to verb, as it were. What is perceived – the women at the bus stop, for instance – seems only a specific catalyst, initiating a break in the scrim of one's daily round. In that moment we're interchangeable with what we see, and at the same time, enacting the self-dispossession that seems to be our phenomenological bedrock, we're at home in the universe.

Moving from the macrocosm of Einstein's theory of relativity to the microcosm of subatomic physics, one learns that if the universe is infinitely large, it's also infinitely small. And at the other extreme, too, a qualitative shift occurs.

In Gary Zukav's lucid study of the new physics, *The Dancing Wu Li Masters*, one learns that the smallest subatomic particle has no "rest mass," no quantifiable substance, that is, and is known to exist only because it reflects the charge of its opposite number, another such particle. Zukav is telling us that the fundamental building block of everything that exists is nonmaterial – rather than being a noun, that is, like light it's known only by what it does.

As light illuminates, a mirror reflects. Could both of these phenomena, in turn, be considered paradigmatic, primary forms of consciousness? Each, that is, is defined by what it reveals outside itself. In other words, at both the small and large ends of our universe, there is a shift from matter, per se, to what is perhaps a primary, very pure form of consciousness.

In my late thirties, I woke from a dream one morning with the image of a drop of ink falling into a glass of water. The following poem came in the wake of the dream:

DAY AND NIGHT

Like a drop
of ink
as it hits

the water –
the whole
glass

going black:
in death
and vision,

decompression –
the soul
united

across
space and
time;

the heart
that was
blind,

a healed thing,
whole.
This

is what
the poet knows
and how he

grows apart.
Oh foolish one,
oblivious

of broken
light:
the one contained

holds the day,
the one apart
the night.

In this poem, written a short time before I got word that my father
was dying, the phenomenon of death and the experience of perception (or vision) are equated. I've puzzled over this in the intervening years since writing it. If one correlates what is said here with
the earlier commentary, it seems to me that the parallel between
death and perception, is, again, self-dispossession. If this event
underlies all matter, dead or alive (as those mirroring subatomic
particles comprise both phenomena), then death itself becomes an
involuntary and permanent enactment of the condition, whereas
vision, while also perhaps involuntary, remains to those of us alive
a fleeting experience. In either instance, in becoming synchronous
with the mirroring action that underlies everything, identity is
eclipsed by the larger common ground: self-dispossession.

INDEX

SOURCES & ACKNOWLEDGMENTS

Grateful acknowledgment is made to the editors and publishers of the publications in which the following pieces – sometimes with different titles or in different form or both – first appeared:

Fielding Dawson: *Dictionary of Literary Biography: Yearbook 2002* (Gale Publishers, 2002) and *Transit* (2002, United Kingdom).

Poets of the Realm: *poetryfoundation.org*, April 22, 2009.

A Fine Romance: *Shambhala Sun*, May 2004.

A Complicated Muse: *American Poetry Review*, Vol. 37. No. 5, September/ October 2008.

Charles Mingus: *Los Angeles Times Book Review*, September 15, 2002.

Andy Warhol: I'll Be Your Mirror: *Andy Warhol by Andy Warhol* (Astrup Fearnley Museum of Modern Art/Skira, 2008).

Occupation Writer: *Contemporary Authors*, Volume 270 (Gale, 2009).

The Driver: Notes on Jack Kerouac: *Ararat*, Volume XXIX, No. 3, Summer 1988.

A Letter to the New York School: *Poetry Project Newsletter*, No. 15, May 1974.

Clark Coolidge and I: *Stations 5*, 1978.

A New York Poet: *New York Times Book Review*, December 14, 1975.

Goodbye to the 1960s: *Village Voice*, January 24, 1977.

Performing Poet: *New York Times Book Review*, April 25, 1976.

Golden Gate: *Village Voice*, May 16, 1977.

Echo Chambers: *Village Voice*, February 23, 1976.

A Breath: *Village Voice*, April 26, 1976.

Reedies: *American Book Review*, Vol. 1, No. 4. October 1978.

Creeley's Novel: *Poetry: A Magazine of Verse*, April 1964.

Sentences: *Lines 4*, March 1965.

Sentences II and Sentences III: *Lines 5*, May 1965.

"Today, May 6th, 1965...": *Elephant*, 1965.

Finlay's Present: *Kulchur 19*, Vol. 5, Autumn 1965.

"Walking I am reading...": *Elephant*, 1965.

A Note on Giacometti: *Joglars 3*, 1965.

A Letter to the Village Voice: *Village Voice*, March 3, 1966.

A Poem of a Life: A 1–12 in *The World* (1969); A 13–21 in *Poetry: A Magazine of Verse*, November 1970.

DESIGN & COMPOSITION BY CARL W. SCABRROUGH